# THE BEGINNER'S GUIDE TO
# Cookie Decorating

T0383476

To Rudy, Emma, and Aidan . . .
This book is possible because of you.
You've allowed me to pursue my passion
and have given me the encouragement to
keep going, no matter what roadblocks
were ahead. Without you, I would not
be where I am today, doing what I love.
Thank you for continuing to support me in
this journey; everything I do is for you.

# THE BEGINNER'S GUIDE TO
# Cookie Decorating

Easy Techniques
and Expert Tips
for Designing and Icing
Colorful Treats

## MARY VALENTINO

# CONTENTS

# INTRODUCTION

When I was a little girl, I used to melt chocolate chip cookies in my yellow-colored Easy-Bake Oven. I never made them from scratch at that age; we just had the store-bought cookies. I'd slide them into the oven, heat them up, and watch them melt. I was so proud of my baking skills and would offer my "baked goods" to anyone who would entertain me.

My grandmother, Maria (whom we called Nonina), was an amazing baker. I would watch her for hours while she prepared cakes and other desserts. She never used any measuring tools. She would just toss in the ingredients while gauging only by eye. The result was always the perfect cake. I hope she knows (from above) that she played a role in where I am today.

My baking journey continued throughout the years, but not the decorated cookies you'll see in this book. I made banana bread, scones, and shortbread—even boxed cakes. I had no idea that an entire world of sugar cookies and royal icing even existed.

In 2013 I was working in the financial industry; it was a stressful environment, and I had no creative outlet. I signed up for Wilton cake-decorating classes at a local art store. The focus was on fondant and buttercream, and I wanted to learn how to create beautiful cakes and cupcakes. But I quickly discovered that working with fondant was not for me. Throughout the classes, we touched on royal icing flowers—I had no idea that it could be used to decorate cookies.

Later that year, I stumbled into the cookie world and I researched everything there was to know about cookie decorating. I spent countless hours learning about royal icing and sugar cookies, reading blog posts, paid tutorials, and everything in between. I experimented with recipes relentlessly until I perfected the ones I use today. I'll admit that it wasn't easy at first to decorate a cookie, but I promise that with time, practice, and patience, you too can master this art.

This book will provide you with everything you need to know to get started on your cookie-decorating journey. You'll find basic recipes, a variety of techniques, step-by-step tutorials, and so much more. I share everything that I've learned over the years, along with tips and tricks for success, so you too can create jaw-dropping creations that are sure to impress.

## Getting Started

Starting a new craft or technique can be overwhelming. I know first-hand how intimidating it was when I started decorating cookies. I've filled this book with my insight and knowledge, including tried-and-tested recipes that will yield perfectly shaped cookies, the must-have tools for your arsenal, how to store and freeze decorated cookies, and so much more.

I address the most frequently asked questions I've received over the years, such as what different types of food colorants are available, what are the differences between luster dusts and edible glitters, and what is the best royal icing consistency to use. The techniques are designed to improve your skills, so make sure to review them before attempting the step-by-step tutorials. If you missed any, they'll be referenced throughout the book.

A few things to remember: The methods and techniques I use in this book are what work best for me. If you find another way to do it, that's okay! Do what works for you. If you're new to cookie decorating, my tips and tricks should be helpful. If you're a skilled cookie artist, you may learn a few things you didn't know, or perhaps you'll be inspired by my designs.

No matter why you're reading this book—to bake for family or friends or start your own cookie business—please remember that you are amazing and talented! Never compare yourself to others. You're unique and you'll find your own decorating style. Be creative, be patient, and keep going. I'm excited for you to start decorating, so let's go!

# BAKING BASICS

Your goal may be to become a skilled cookie decorator, but to do that you have to start with a great canvas: cookies. This chapter introduces you to essential baking equipment such as rolling pins, parchment paper, and cooling racks. Each item plays a vital role in the process and helps ensure your cookies are as delicious as can be. I've also included my tried-and-true recipes for sugar, gingerbread, shortbread, and chocolate cookies—something for every taste and season. These recipes have been perfected over the years and hold their shape while baking. All they'll need is royal icing and your creativity.

# TOOLS FOR BAKING

Before you begin baking, make sure that your kitchen is equipped with these tools. Having these will ensure that the baking process goes smoothly.

## Baking Sheets and Liners

I prefer using a 21" × 15" (53 × 38 cm) aluminum baking pan, which can hold up to 12 medium-size cookies. You can also use a flat-edge cookie sheet with small grips on one or both sides for easy handling.

These silicone sheets line the bottom of baking pans and can be used in place of parchment paper. They're reusable, nonstick, clean up easily, and are usually double-sided. Silicone liners provide consistent and even heat distribution.

Baking pans can also be lined with parchment paper, which is nonstick and grease resistant. I use this paper to roll out my dough, but usually don't use it to line my baking pans because I find it doesn't provide for even baking.

Not pictured: Plastic wrap is used to wrap disks of dough for chilling.

## Rolling Pins and Dowels

Several types of rolling pins are available, including tapered and straight, and with and without handles. I prefer a 20" (51 cm) straight rolling pin, which works well for large batches of dough. I also use ¼" (6 mm) wooden dowels; placing them on either side of the dough while rolling it out ensures an even and consistent roll.

## Assorted Baking Tools

**Cups** and **spoons** are used to measure ingredients for baking and can be made out of metal, plastic, or other materials.

A **cookie spatula** is ideal for picking up cookies from the baking sheet and transferring them to the cooling rack.

**Wire cooling racks** are designed to allow airflow to circulate around the cookies during the cooling process.

A **handheld rasp grater** (a common brand is Microplane) gently sands bumpy or overbaked edges off of cookies.

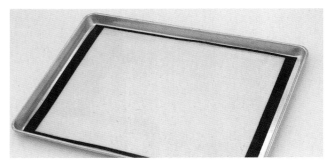

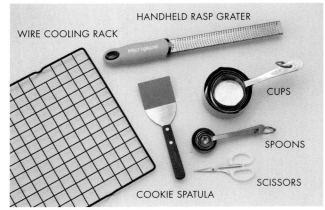

Not pictured: A silicone spatula is a food-grade tool that is used to mix ingredients and scrape dough and icing off the sides of mixing bowls.

Scraping icing over stencils and other surfaces is easier with a dough scraper or icing scraper, typically made of durable plastic that has a little flex and a thin edge.

## Cookie cutters

Cutters are used to cut dough into different shapes and sizes, and can be made of metal or plastic. Always follow the manufacturer's instructions for cleaning to avoid damaging the cutters.

The advent of 3-D laser printers has made it possible to purchase any cookie-cutter shape imaginable. Some businesses offer custom shapes as well. Resources can be found online.

## Electric Mixers

Stand mixers are large, heavy-duty mixers with powerful motors that typically have add-on attachments such as whisks and dough hooks for various types of mixing and kneading. I use the paddle attachment to make cookie dough and royal icing. If you don't have a stand mixer, a hand mixer will work.

# COOKIE RECIPES

Back in the early days of cookie decorating, I tested dozens of cookie recipes. Some tasted great but spread so much that the cut shapes were no longer recognizable. Finding recipes for cookies that are delicious and hold their shape while baking can be challenging (it was for me, anyway!).

The sugar cookie recipes and gingerbread recipe in this book took me a while to perfect. I wanted a simple cookie that was delicious, had a mild sweetness, and didn't spread. These recipes provide a great base for decorating with royal icing.

I've also included my shortbread recipe. This one does spread, so it may not be ideal for decorating with royal icing. But it tastes so good that I had to include it in the book as a bonus. When I appeared on Food Network's *Christmas Cookie Challenge*, one of the judges said, "It just melts in my mouth . . . the texture is great. I think this is the perfect shortbread!" You be the judge.

Remember that ovens vary, so temperatures and baking times may need to be adjusted.

# SUGAR COOKIES

This is my go-to recipe for cookies that are great for decorating. They offer the perfect base for icing, since they don't spread while baking. Tasty and not too sweet, these cookies are crunchy on the outside and soft on the inside. I love to eat them warm out of the oven with a cup of coffee.

MAKES 3 DOZEN 3" (7.5 CM) COOKIES

2 cups (454 g) unsalted butter, softened

2 cups (400 g) granulated sugar

2 large eggs (cold)

1 teaspoon salt

1 tablespoon (15 ml) pure vanilla extract

6 cups (750 g) all-purpose flour

1. In the bowl of an electric stand mixer fitted with a paddle attachment, cream the butter and sugar together until pale yellow in color, approximately 5 minutes. Scrape down the sides of the bowl.

2. Beat in the eggs. Scrape down the sides of the bowl. Add the salt and vanilla and mix on low speed until combined.

*(continued)*

3. Add the flour on low speed until well combined. When the dough pulls away from the side of the bowl, it's ready.

   **Note:** If using a hand mixer, the dough may become too heavy to handle and mix. Mix the butter, sugar, eggs, salt, and vanilla as per steps 1 and 2. Then, manually knead in the flour until mixed well.

4. Separate the dough into two equal-size balls.

5. Place one ball on a sheet of parchment paper and place two ¼" (6 mm) dowels on either side, about 2" (5 cm) away from the edges (5A). Place another sheet of parchment paper on top of the dough (5B).

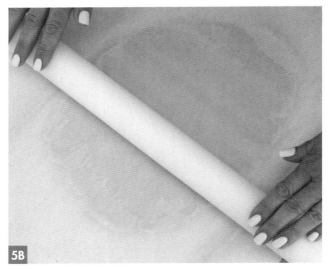

6. Roll out the dough, using a straight rolling pin, making sure that you're rolling over the dough and the dowels. This will ensure you roll out an even slab of dough.

7. Repeat steps 5 and 6 with the second ball of dough.

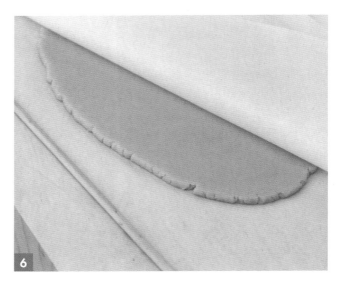

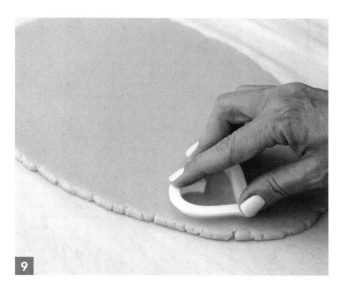

9

10

8. Slide the dough with both parchment sheets onto a flat board, place it inside a large zip-top bag, and refrigerate for at least 1 hour, and up to overnight. The dough should be chilled prior to cutting. If desired, you can freeze the dough at this point (see box, below).

9. Remove the chilled dough from the bag and cut shapes with a cookie cutter. If using plastic cutters, wait a few minutes before cutting the shapes as the dough may be too hard and could possibly damage the cutters.

10. With a cookie spatula, transfer the cut cookies to a baking sheet lined with a silicone mat or parchment paper. Leave at least 1½" (4 cm) of space between each cookie. Place the filled baking sheets in the freezer for at least 30 minutes. This step is optional, but chilling the cookies in the freezer before baking can help prevent them from spreading.

11. While the dough is chilling, preheat the oven to 350°F (180°C or gas mark 4).

12. Place the baking sheet in the oven and bake 14 to 16 minutes, or until the edges turn golden brown. Remove the cookies from the oven and leave on the baking sheet for 10 minutes, then transfer them to a cooling rack.

*(continued)*

## FREEZING DOUGH

This cookie dough can be made ahead of time and frozen until ready to bake. Prepare the dough as instructed and place the rolled dough between sheets of parchment paper, on top of a sturdy board or sheet. Seal the sheets in a large zip-top bag and store in the freezer. Take sheets out as you need them and thaw until they're firm, but not too hard. The dough can be frozen for up to 3 months.

Create perfect edges on cookies by using a handheld grater, such as a Microplane. Gently scrape any edges that are overbaked or uneven. This will work on straight or curved edges.

## TIPS FOR SUCCESSFUL COOKIES

Try to only re-roll scraps twice. Re-rolled dough doesn't bake up as nicely. You might notice misshapen pieces and bubbles on the surface, and cookies can become denser and tougher.

However, most bakers don't want excess dough to go to waste. When you re-roll the dough, place it in the refrigerator for 15 minutes to allow it to firm up before cutting. After cutting the shapes, you can pick them up with your hands and transfer to the baking sheet, since the dough will be a bit stiffer and won't bend or warp. If bubbles appear on the surface after baking, use a fondant smoother (found online or in some specialty baking or large craft stores) to gently flatten them out while the cookies are still warm. If decorating the cookies with royal icing, that will cover most of the surface also.

# MARBLING DOUGH

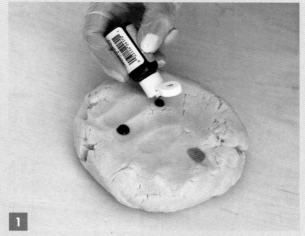

Coloring your dough is a great way to add a punch of excitement to your cookies. You can skip icing them altogether, or partially decorate them. Either way, this technique is sure to add a wow factor.

1. Put on a pair of food-safe gloves and add a drop each of the three shades of gel food coloring to a flattened ball of sugar cookie dough. I used blue, pink, and yellow.

2. Knead the dough by hand a few times until you achieve the desired effect, which is up to you. I went for a tie-dye effect, but keep in mind that the more you knead the dough, the more the colors will blend.

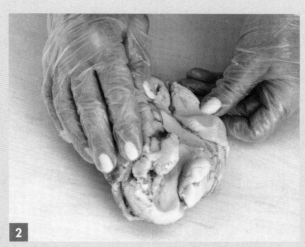

3. Roll the dough to ¼" (6 mm) thickness and follow the steps for cutting and baking sugar cookies (see page 13).

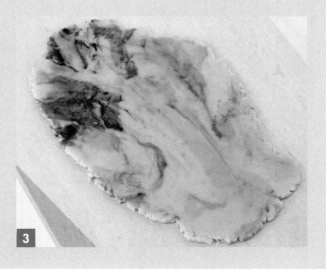

# CHOCOLATE COOKIES

This basic chocolate cookie recipe is simple to make and has a mild chocolate flavor. The cookies are delicious to eat on their own, but they also make the perfect base for decorating, since they hold their shape while baking.

MAKES 3 DOZEN 3" (7.5 CM) COOKIES

| |
|---|
| 2 cups (454 g) unsalted butter |
| 2 cups (400 g) granulated sugar |
| 2 tablespoons (30 ml) pure vanilla extract |
| ½ teaspoon salt |
| 2 eggs |
| 5 cups (625 g) all-purpose flour, plus a little extra for kneading |
| ½ cup (60 g) cocoa powder |

1. In a mixer fitted with the paddle attachment, cream together the butter, sugar, vanilla, and salt until smooth, about 3 minutes. Scrape down the sides of the bowl, then add the eggs and mix well.

2. Scrape down the sides of the bowl again. Slowly add the cocoa powder and flour. Mix until a soft dough forms. Dust your hands with flour and knead the dough in the bowl until smooth.

3. Separate the dough into two equal-size balls. Wrap the dough pieces in clear plastic wrap and place in the refrigerator for 20 minutes to chill.

4. Remove the dough from the refrigerator and dust a piece of parchment paper with flour. Place one ball of dough in the center of the parchment paper, dust some flour on top.

5. Place two ¼" (6 mm) wooden dowels on either side of the dough, 2" (5 cm) away from the edges. Place another sheet of parchment paper on top. Roll out the dough using a straight rolling pin, making sure that you're rolling over the dough and the dowels. This will ensure an even slab of dough.

6. Repeat steps 4 and 5 with the second ball of dough.

7. Slide the dough, still on the parchment sheet, onto a flat board. Place the dough inside a large zip-top bag and refrigerate for at least 1 hour.

8. While the dough is chilling, preheat the oven to 350°F (180°C or gas mark 4).

9. Remove the dough from the refrigerator, cut out the shapes, and place the cookies on a baking sheet lined with parchment paper or a silicone mat. Leave at least 1" (2.5 cm) between each cookie.

10. Bake the cookies on the middle rack for 10 to 12 minutes. After removing the cookies from the oven, leave them on the baking sheet for 10 minutes before moving them to a cooling rack. Once the cookies are completely cool they can be decorated.

# GINGERBREAD COOKIES

I use this recipe for gingerbread every year during the holidays. My son loves eating them undecorated and warm out of the oven, although they pair perfectly with royal icing. Once cooled, the cookies have crisp edges and a soft center. The cinnamon and spice aromas are a delight to the senses.

MAKES 2 DOZEN 3" (7.5 CM) COOKIES

3 cups (375 g) all-purpose flour

½ teaspoon salt

1 tablespoon (15 g) ground cinnamon

4 teaspoons (20 g) ground ginger

½ teaspoon allspice

½ teaspoon baking soda

¾ cup (170 g) unsalted butter, melted

¾ cup (150 g) lightly packed brown sugar

1 egg

½ cup (170 g) fancy molasses

1. Stir together the flour, salt, cinnamon, ginger, allspice, and baking soda in a large mixing bowl. Set aside.

2. In another large mixing bowl, beat the butter with the brown sugar on medium speed for 2 minutes. Beat in the egg and molasses.

3. Add the molasses mixture to the flour mixture, using a spatula to scrape the molasses from the sides of the bowl. Beat on low speed until the flour is combined and the dough is soft and no longer sticky. Form the dough into a disk and cover it in plastic wrap. Refrigerate for at least 30 minutes or until firm.

4. While the dough is chilling, preheat the oven to 350°F (180°C or gas mark 4).

5. Remove the dough from the refrigerator and dust a piece of parchment paper with flour. Place the dough in the center of the parchment paper and dust the top of the dough with flour.

6. Place two ¼" (6 mm) wooden dowels on either side of the dough, 2" (5 cm) away from the edges. Place another sheet of parchment paper on top. Roll out the dough using a straight rolling pin, making sure that you're rolling over the dough and the dowels. This will ensure an even slab of dough.

7. Cut out the shapes using cookie cutters and place the cookies on a baking sheet lined with parchment paper or a silicone mat.

8. Bake on the center rack for 8 to 10 minutes, or until the edges are deep brown and firm. Remove the cookies from the oven and leave them on the baking sheet for at least 5 minutes before transferring them to a wire rack to cool.

9. Store the cookies in an airtight container in a cool setting for up to 1 week. The cookies can also be frozen in an airtight container for up to 1 month. Eat them plain, dipped in chocolate, or decorated with royal icing.

# SHORTBREAD COOKIES

This is one of my favorite cookies to bake around the holidays. They are buttery, crisp to the bite, and filled with melt-in-your-mouth deliciousness. The cookies can be used as a base to decorate with royal icing, but they do spread a little while baking and may not be ideal for all designs.

MAKES 4½ DOZEN 2" (5 CM) COOKIES

2 cups (454 g) salted butter

1 cup (125 g) powdered sugar

½ cup (65 g) cornstarch

3 cups (375 g) all-purpose flour

1 teaspoon vanilla extract

½ cup (118 g) sanding sugar

1. Preheat the oven to 350°F (180°C or gas mark 4).

2. In a mixer fitted with the paddle attachment, whip the butter on low to medium speed, occasionally scraping down the sides of the bowl. Continue to whip until the butter is pale yellow in color, 3 to 4 minutes.

3. Add the powdered sugar and mix on medium speed until well combined. Add the cornstarch and mix on medium speed until well combined. Add the flour and mix on medium speed until well combined. Add the vanilla and mix until combined.

4. Pour some sanding sugar onto a small plate.

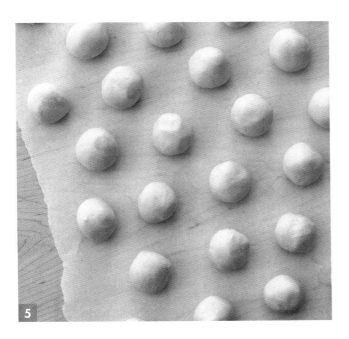

5. Roll the dough into 1¼" (3 cm) balls (you can make them smaller or larger depending on the size of finished cookie you prefer).

6. Press each ball into the sanding sugar, using two fingers, so one side of the cookie is covered in sugar. The cookie should be approximately ½" (1.3 cm) in height.

7. Place the round, flattened dough balls on a baking sheet at least 1½" (4 cm) apart to allow room for the cookies to spread while baking. Bake on the top rack for 6 to 7 minutes, then place the baking sheet on the bottom rack for another 6 to 7 minutes. Remove from the oven when the bottoms of the cookies are golden brown. Allow the cookies to cool on the baking sheets for 10 minutes, then move them to cooling racks to cool completely.

8. The cookies can be stored in an airtight container for up to 2 weeks.

### ROLLING TIPS

If the dough is too sticky to roll into balls, place it in the refrigerator, covered with plastic wrap, for about 10 minutes until it firms up. If you choose to roll and cut the cookies, note that the dough will spread and the shapes may not be as defined. Place the dough on a sheet of parchment paper with two ⅜" (1 cm) dowels on either side, and place another sheet of parchment on top. Roll the dough to the height of the dowels. Place the rolled dough in the refrigerator to chill for at least 1 hour. Since this is a soft dough, chilling will help in the cutting process. Place the cut cookies on a baking sheet and follow the baking instructions in step 7.

# 2

# DECORATING BASICS

Perfecting royal icing is the key to making the most beautifully decorated cookies. In this chapter you'll learn how to make a variety of consistencies used to pipe and fill cookie designs. Decorating tools are included here as well, and while that world is vast, amassing the basics shouldn't be an intimidating process. You'll also get an introduction to using colorants and some fun specialty ingredients, such as edible glitter and luster dust, sanding sugar, and sprinkles.

The beginner-friendly icing and piping techniques will teach you how to create easy designs that you can use in a number of ways, which you'll see later in the cookie projects. Give yourself time to develop your skills—no one becomes a proficient cookie artist overnight. Enjoy the process as you build muscle memory while creating wet-on-wet motifs, brushed embroidery, a woven effect, hand painting, and more. You'll be amazed at how these achievable techniques will elevate your cookies and make them the star of any occasion.

# DECORATING TOOLS

Having the right tools can make the decorating process easier, but figuring out what you need may be overwhelming. I've tried and tested about every tool over the years, so I've put together a list of items I consider to be must-haves in a cookie artist's arsenal.

**Disposable piping bags** are a necessity for any cookie artist, since they hold the royal icing that's used to decorate cookies. The bags can be used with or without piping tips.

A **spatula** is used to scrape down the bowl while mixing the icing.

This pointy **scribe tool** is invaluable for cookie decorators and can be used in many ways: to pop pesky air bubbles in icing, spread icing into corners, and etch designs into icing or onto an uniced cookie.

The two-in-one tool (also known as a **"boo-boo stick"** in the cookie world) is used to fix mistakes on cookies and it's an essential tool in your decorating arsenal. Use the flat edge to scrape off unwanted royal icing from the cookies.

A small pair of **scissors** comes in handy for cutting the tip of the piping bags.

## Piping Tips

Tips can be made of metal or plastic and come in a wide variety of shapes and sizes. Use tips for specialty designs, such as flowers and leaves. Small round tips (numbers 1.5, 2, or 3) can be used if you're not comfortable using tipless bags to pipe designs.

From left to right: tipless piping bag, spatula, decorative scribe tool, basic scribe tool, boo-boo stick, scissors

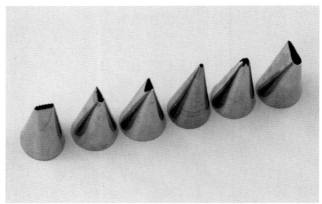

Piping tips, from left to right: basketweave #47, Wilton small petal #102, Wilton leaf #352, Wilton round #2, open star #14, Wilton petal #104

## Mixing Bowls

Small bowls are convenient for separating and mixing small batches of royal icing.

## Food-safe Paintbrushes

Use food-safe brushes to add painted effects with gel food colorants on royal icing, to apply petal dust on fondant, and more. Brushes are also used for icing techniques such as brushed embroidery. I recommend having an assortment of brushes in multiple sizes on hand. The brush size typically depends on the size of the cutter and the designs.

## Tweezers

Rubber-tipped tweezers allow for precise placement of sprinkles.

## Spray Bottle

A plastic trigger spray bottle filled with water can be used to add small amounts of water to icing to thin it to the right consistency.

## Tabletop Fan

A small tabletop fan is handy for speeding up the drying time of iced cookies. When used immediately after flooding cookies with royal icing, it helps prevent craters from forming in the icing and creates a sheen on the surface when fully dry.

I usually use a fan to crust over sections of the cookies in 15-minute intervals; the cookie is crusted over when the surface of the icing begins to harden. If the base layer of icing needs to be completely dry, I'll let the freshly iced cookie sit in front of the fan for at least 30 minutes. After that, I'll allow the icing to air-dry for the specified number of hours for that technique. Cookies should dry uncovered.

# SPECIALTY INGREDIENTS

The items in this category are usually found in baking supply shops or large craft stores. Glitters and dusts will add a shiny, sparkly, or metallic finish to cookies and kick your designs up a notch. Edible ink markers are helpful for drawing lines on bare cookies or fully dry royal icing as a guide for piping additional icing, such as outlines or details.

## Edible Luster Dust

These pearlescent dusts add a colorful shine to royal icing when applied dry or mixed with an alcohol medium for a metallic finish.

### DRY APPLICATION

The royal icing base must be completely dry before applying the luster dust.

1. Scoop some luster dust into the well of a paint palette. Dip a food-grade angled paintbrush into the dust and tap the excess dust off the bristles.

2. If dry dusting a large surface, apply the dust in a back-and-forth motion. If creating facial features such as rosy cheeks, use a round brush and apply the dust in a circular motion.

Edible luster dust

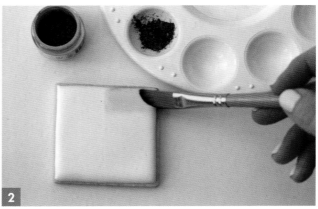

## WET APPLICATION

The royal icing base must be completely dry before applying the luster dust.

1. Squeeze a drop of clear alcohol with a high alcohol content (such as Everclear or Spirytus Vodka) or clear extract into the luster dust using a pipette or dropper. Add one drop at a time to ensure it doesn't liquefy too much. The ratio should be about two parts dust to one part alcohol.

2. Use an angled paintbrush to mix the powder and alcohol well.

3. Paint the mixture directly onto the icing surface. For a deeper color with more coverage, wait a few minutes for the first coat to dry, then apply a second coat.

4. The finished look should be metallic and shiny when using a high-content alcohol. If a clear extract is used, the finish may not be as shiny.

High-content alcohol evaporates quickly, so it won't sit on the surface for a long time. This prevents the royal icing surface from melting and creating a dull finish.

## Edible Glitter and Sparkle Dust

Add bling to royal icing with edible glitter, which can be applied with a special pump bottle designed to spray a fine, even layer of glitter. Since the glitter needs moisture to adhere to the icing, it's best to use it with royal icing that has just crusted over and is still tacky. Spraying glitter directly onto fresh icing results in less shine, because the glitter particles sink into the icing.

1.  Apply stiff-consistency royal icing to a cookie using a spatula.

2.  Spray edible glitter or sparkle dust directly onto the royal icing.

3.  The result is a beautiful sparkly finish.

Edible glitter/sparkle dust

To apply edible glitter or sparkle dust to flooded royal icing, place the freshly flooded cookie in front of a fan to dry for 10 minutes, then spray the dust directly onto the royal icing.

## Edible Petal Dust

This product creates a deep matte finish on royal icing or fondant. Dusting dry powder onto molded fondant accents adds depth and dimension to sugar work such as flowers and leaves.

1. Dip a small, round food-safe paintbrush into the petal dust and blot the excess on a paper towel or tap it back into the jar.

2. Brush the dust into the crevices of the fondant leaf. Add more to deepen the color.

3. Repeat the steps for the fondant flower, brushing between the petals to add dimension.

Edible petal dust

In this side-by-side comparison, note the difference between the plain fondant flower and leaves on the left and the petal-dust-enhanced flower on the right.

## Sprinkles, Nonpareils, and Sanding Sugar

Embellish your cookies and any sweet treats with colorful sprinkles that come in an array of shapes and solid and mixed colors.

## Fondant Accents

Most people think of fondant, a rolled icing, as a smooth covering on a cake. While I mostly use royal icing to decorate cookies, I like to incorporate molded fondant accents to add texture and dimension, such as florals (see Fondant Accents with Silicone Molds, page 82). You can make fondant from scratch or purchase ready-made fondant in specialty baking supply shops as well as some craft stores.

Sprinkles

Sanding sugar

Edible markers/food pens

## Edible Ink Pens and Markers

These pens come in multiple colors and fine or thick nibs and can be used to draw on dried royal icing as well as bare cookies. Thin nibs are great for adding fine details such as eyelashes and lips. The pens can also be used to outline shapes on cookies prior to icing. I don't recommend using fine tips to outline on bare cookies as they can damage the nib. Thicker tips are best to draw on bare cookies. Be sure to wipe the tip of your food pens on a paper towel after drawing on bare cookies to avoid damage and drying out. Make sure the royal icing is completely dry before writing or drawing, or the pen can puncture and damage the icing.

Lightly sketching a design with an edible ink pen makes it easier to create designs using different techniques.

# ROYAL ICING RECIPE

Royal icing is a frosting made of icing sugar and meringue powder, and sometimes flavorings are added. Because it dries hard, it's a preferred choice for decorative cookies. You'll use a variety of consistencies of royal icing throughout the book for the various techniques, as well as for decorative floral accents.

DECORATES APPROXIMATELY 4 DOZEN
3" (7.5 CM) COOKIES

8 tablespoons (98 g) meringue powder (found in baking supply stores)

¾ cup (180 ml) water

8 cups (1 kg) powdered sugar

1 teaspoon vanilla extract (I use Wilton Imitation Clear Vanilla Extract so it doesn't darken the icing)

1. Add the meringue powder to a small bowl. Add the water and mix well with a paddle attachment. The texture should be smooth and not grainy.

2. Sift the powdered sugar before adding it to the bowl of an electric mixer fitted with the paddle attachment or a large mixing bowl. Add the meringue mixture. Combine on low speed for 1 minute. Scrape down the sides of the bowl.

3. Add the vanilla and continue to mix on medium-low speed for 5 minutes, scraping down the bowl as needed. The icing is ready when it turns bright white and is thick enough to hold a stiff peak.

This is how the icing should look when it's ready—glossy and able to hold a stiff peak. Note that if you don't use clear vanilla, the icing may look off-white.

# STORING ROYAL ICING AND ICED COOKIES

Royal icing begins to set quickly when exposed to air. Follow these instructions for storing it properly so it does not harden.

## Storing Royal Icing

Once the icing is out of the mixing bowl, cover it immediately. Portion out the required amounts into small bowls and cover them until they're ready to be tinted. Alternatively, you can leave the icing in the mixing bowl, then soak a large cloth or tea towel with water, wring it out to remove excess liquid, and use it to cover the mixing bowl. If the cloth dries out, repeat the process. If you allow the towel to dry, the icing will begin to harden.

Icing can be stored in the refrigerator in an airtight container. After transferring the icing to the container, lightly press a piece of plastic wrap onto the surface and cover it with the lid. Icing can be stored in the refrigerator up to 2 weeks and in the freezer for up to 6 months.

For some techniques, you'll need to store icing while decorating the cookies. Icing can remain in the piping bags; place the bags in an airtight container and store in the refrigerator. Later or the following day, remove the bags from the refrigerator and allow them to come to room temperature. Before using, massage the bags with your hands to remix the icing. This will also remix icing if it separated while chilling. If massaging the bag doesn't bring the icing back to a smooth consistency, you may need to place the icing back in a mixing bowl and mix it with a spatula.

Alternatively, you can empty the icing from piping bags into a mixing bowl, place a lid on the bowl, and place it in the refrigerator. Later or the following day, allow it to come to room temperature and remix it with a spatula.

If freezing the icing, allow it to come to room temperature and follow the instructions above if the icing has separated.

## Storing Iced Cookies

Sugar cookies that have been decorated with royal icing can be frozen. I used to do this all the time when I made custom cookies. Once the cookies are completely dry, package them in clear, sealable cellophane bags or seal them with a heat-sealing machine (available online). Carefully stack them in a large airtight container and place it in the freezer for up to 1 month.

Take the cookies out of the freezer 1 to 2 days prior to eating them. Remove the container carefully and place it on a countertop. Don't remove the lid or you risk getting condensation in the container, which can damage the cookies. Allow the cookies to thaw completely inside the container overnight. The lid can be safely removed the following day. Your cookies will remain fresh and tasty, and no one will know they were frozen.

I recommend doing a trial run of freezing and thawing a few cookies to make sure you're comfortable with the process and happy with the outcome before you need to freeze dozens of cookies for an event.

# COLORING ICING

Several options are available for coloring royal icing, including liquid colorants, liquid gels, gel paste (also called gel), powders (also referred to as dusts), and natural food colorings. With the abundance of products available from a variety of manufacturers, deciding what to use can be overwhelming. I've worked with all of the colorants mentioned and find that some offer better results than others. Read on for more details on all of them.

If you've used clear vanilla extract to flavor the royal icing, the end product will be white. If the flavoring (such as pure vanilla extract) is tinted brown, the icing will likely be off-white or ivory. Since most of the icing you'll use will be tinted, starting with off-white icing won't be a concern. Royal icing can be brightened with a liquid or dust whitener.

## Types of Colorants

**DUST OR POWDER PIGMENTS** typically come in small jars. They're usually made with synthetic coloring and no water, glycerin, or corn syrup. Small amounts of dust are very concentrated and allow you to attain dark or vibrant colors. They also won't change an icing's consistency or alter the taste. A little goes a long way, so always start with a small scoop of the product.

**LIQUID GEL** is a thick, gel-like liquid that's usually available in small squeeze bottles. This synthetic coloring has a water, glycerin, or corn syrup base. Since this is a highly concentrated colorant, only a little is needed to create vibrant colors. Liquid gels are easy to use and mix nicely into royal icing.

**GEL PASTE (ALSO CALLED GEL)** colorants usually come in little pots or jars and are thicker than liquid gels. Like liquid gel, it consists of synthetic coloring with a water, glycerin, or corn syrup base. These are also extremely concentrated, so you don't need a lot to achieve vibrant colors. Royal icing can easily be oversaturated with gels, so use a toothpick to collect a small amount of colorant from the jar, adding more as needed. Always use a fresh toothpick when collecting more gel from the jar, as reusing the same one can contaminate the contents.

**LIQUID FOOD COLORING** consists of a synthetic dye in a water base and can be found in most grocery stores in small squeeze bottles. This is an inexpensive option for coloring royal icing, and the colors are less concentrated than other colorants, making them perfect for creating pale shades. Since it would take several bottles to achieve deep, dark shades in large batches of icing, this type of colorant isn't typically used for cookie decorating.

**NATURAL FOOD COLORINGS** are made from plant sources, such as fruits and vegetables, and are great for those who want to avoid synthetic dyes or who have allergies. The liquids come in small squeeze bottles and are usually more expensive than the other types of food colorants. The colors produced are more muted than gels and dusts, so a significant amount of colorant may be needed to achieve deep shades.

From left to right: dust/powder pigment, liquid gel, gel, gel paste, liquid food coloring, natural food coloring

## Using Colorants

Try different types of colorants to see which ones you like best and produce the shades you want. Mix up a batch of royal icing (see page 34) and divide it into small bowls for testing.

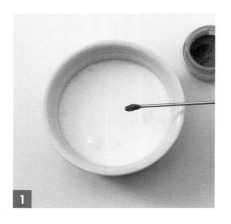  

### DUST OR POWDER PIGMENTS

1. Use a mini spoon to scoop a small amount of dust out of the jar and add it to the icing.

2. The dust is activated with water. Use a small spray bottle to mist some water over the top of the icing.

3. Use a spatula to thoroughly mix the icing in a circular motion. Scrape down the sides of the bowl as needed.

4. The dust usually dissolves easily, resulting in a vibrant and rich color.

## LIQUID FOOD COLORING

1.  Invert a bottle over the bowl of icing and squeeze gently. Add color drop by drop, stirring well after each addition, until you achieve the desired shade.

2.  Use a spatula to thoroughly mix the icing in a circular motion. Scrape down the sides of the bowl as needed. Add water to thin the icing if necessary.

3.  The color mixes easily and produces a beautiful pastel hue.

 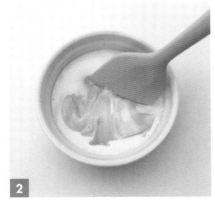 

## LIQUID GEL

1.  Squeeze some of the liquid gel into the icing. Since this product is thicker than liquid food coloring, you'll need more pressure when squeezing the bottle—but be careful not to release too much gel and oversaturate the icing. For paler shades, remove the lid and use a toothpick to collect a small amount of colorant.

2.  Use a spatula to thoroughly mix the icing in a circular motion. Scrape down the sides of the bowl as needed. Add water to thin the icing if necessary.

3.  The result is a bright and vivid color.

## GEL PASTE

1. Use a toothpick to collect a small amount of gel from the jar and dip it into the royal icing.

2. Use a spatula to thoroughly mix the icing in a circular motion. Scrape down the sides of the bowl as needed. To add more gel, use a fresh toothpick and repeat the process.

3. Make sure all the colorant is dissolved in the icing.

## NATURAL FOOD COLORING

1. Squeeze a drop of color into the royal icing.

2. Use a spatula to thoroughly mix the icing in a circular motion. Scrape down the sides of the bowl as needed. Continue to add color drop by drop until the desired shade is reached.

3. This vivid color was achieved by adding numerous drops of the natural colorant.

# ROYAL ICING CONSISTENCIES

You've just mixed up a fresh batch of royal icing and are eager to start decorating. After following the recipe (see page 34), you notice that the finished icing is as thick as buttercream—this is the way it's supposed to be. So how do you achieve a smooth surface on your cookies? Read on and I'll break it down for you.

Throughout the book, you'll work with four main icing consistencies: stiff, piping, medium, and flood. The basic recipe for royal icing will be at a stiff consistency just after mixing. Piping consistency is a little bit thinner, followed by medium, and then flood, which is the thinnest consistency. How to create the various consistencies and when best to use them is explained later in this chapter.

If you're new to cookie decorating, you may think that achieving the perfect icing consistency can be the trickiest and most complex part of the process. I always say that consistency is key! If the icing is too thin, it will run off the sides of the cookies. If it's too stiff, it won't settle properly and the surface will be lumpy. Getting the right consistency is imperative and determines the success of your designs, but it's not that difficult to achieve.

The process includes adding water to the just-made stiff icing and adjusting the amount of water for different decorating techniques. Many cookie decorators search for a magic recipe that will allow them to create that satisfying, smooth surface. But really, there isn't one—it all comes down to tweaking the amount of water.

Describing icing consistencies can be challenging, since it must be seen and felt; how does it settle and smooth out in a bowl? I'll share what I've learned over the years, and this information will help you achieve success. There will be some trial and error, but nailing the consistency will make all the difference in your designs. With patience and persistence, you'll perfect it.

## Thinning the Icing

The simplest way to thin royal icing is to add water using a spray bottle. Spray a small amount of water in a bowl of icing, mix it with a spatula, and repeat until you get the desired consistency (continue reading for more information on royal icing consistencies).

After years of decorating, I can gauge the consistency by eye, but that didn't happen overnight—repetition and determination got me there. Don't get discouraged if you haven't perfected the technique early in your journey. With time and patience, you will.

## Thickening the Icing

At some point, you may have to alter flood-consistency icing (see page 47) back to a stiffer consistency. You may have added too much water or need to convert flood icing back to a medium or piping consistency to create fine lines or small details. To do this, add more stiff-consistency icing to the thinner icing and mix until you reach the desired consistency (this is my preferred method). Or add powdered sugar, 1 teaspoon at a time, and mix until you have the consistency you want.

If you need piping and flood icings in the same color, add the desired amount of royal icing to one mixing bowl. A fresh batch of icing should have a thick consistency. Add a little bit of water and thin it to the thickest piping consistency you need. Add color to the icing. Coloring and mixing the icing is easier to do when the icing is thinner. Transfer the desired amount for another batch of icing to a second bowl to continue to thin it further to a flood consistency.

If you've added color to the icing, it will lighten when more icing or powdered sugar is added. To maintain the original shade, add more colorant.

## Achieving Different Icing Consistencies

As explained previously, four main icing consistencies are used in cookie decorating: stiff, piping, medium, and flood.

I prefer using one consistency of icing for outlining designs and for flooding or filling them (see page 47) when decorating most cookies; some decorators prefer to outline cookies with thicker icing and flood with a thinner one. I like a seamless finish that doesn't show the outline on the finished cookies. I'll use two consistencies for some types of cookies, depending on the designs and shapes I'm working with. A thicker-consistency icing creates sharp, pointed corners on a square cookie, for example, but a thinner icing would lose its shape when piped. As you work through the tutorials in this book, I'll explain why I use two consistencies for some cookies. Do what works best for you—there is no right or wrong way.

When a cookie design calls for several techniques, you may need multiple icing consistencies to achieve various effects. For example, a ballerina with a ruffled skirt requires both medium- and stiff-consistency royal icing—medium for small sections such as the arms and face, and stiff for the ruffles. The medium consistency creates a puffy surface and the icing won't spill into surrounding sections, and stiff icing will ensure that the tutu holds its shape. This will make more sense as we talk about the four main consistencies used in cookie decorating.

Here I share how to achieve the four consistencies.

Icing consistencies, from left to right: stiff, piping, medium, and flood

One way to tell whether icing is the correct consistency is with a consistency count. Cut a line through the icing in the bowl with a knife. The time in seconds that it takes for the icing to seam back together is a good indication that you have achieved the right consistency. The amount of time is noted in each consistency.

## STIFF

Icing that's just been mixed has a stiff consistency that holds a peak. It won't flow out of a piping bag and it's not ideal for icing the base of a cookie. The look and consistency of this icing is similar to cake frosting.

You cannot count stiff icing in seconds; it does not settle when you cut through it with a knife. The icing doesn't settle within itself.

**Best for:** Making petalled flowers, leaves, ruffles, stenciling, brushed embroidery, and shell borders

## PIPING

This consistency is comparable to that of toothpaste and should flow nicely out of a piping bag. To achieve this consistency, use a spray bottle to spritz some water in a bowl of stiff-consistency icing and mix it in. The icing should create a soft peak once piped, with the peak quickly losing its form once it settles. If the icing snaps or breaks while piping, it's too thick and more water should be added. If piped lines don't keep their form, the icing is too thin and will need to be thickened (see page 44).

**Best for:** Outlining shapes with sharp edges/corners and piping letters
**Icing consistency count:** 25 seconds

---

### A NOTE FOR BEGINNERS ON ICING CONSISTENCY

Although I prefer using one consistency for both outlining and flooding cookies, I don't suggest that combination if you're new to royal icing. Using a medium consistency to outline and a flood consistency to fill will be easier to work with while you're learning. As you become more familiar and comfortable with the consistencies, you can create a single consistency to use for most designs that's somewhere between medium and flood.

## MEDIUM

Add more water with a spray bottle to piping-consistency icing to achieve a medium consistency. Always add the water in increments, mix thoroughly, and add more if necessary. The texture should be between flood (see right) and piping (see opposite) consistency. This allows you to outline and fill shapes with the same icing, eliminating the separation between them.

**Best for:** Filling in small sections, preventing dips in the design, royal icing transfers (see page 61), script writing, bead borders, flowers with flat petals, a puffy look
**Icing consistency count:** 12 to 15 seconds

## FLOOD

Add enough water to stiff-consistency icing so it's a little runny but doesn't lose its shape. When spread on a cookie, it should stay on top, not run off the sides. If it does, the icing is too thin and air bubbles may appear. Add more stiff-consistency icing to the mixture and stir.

**Best for:** Filling larger cookie surfaces, wet-on-wet technique (see page 58), and flooding large cookies
**Icing consistency count:** 5 to 10 seconds

# TOOLS FOR ICING

## Piping Tips Versus Tipless Piping Bags

When I started decorating cookies, I worked with reusable pastry bags, along with a piping tip and coupler (this connects the tip to the bag). Tips come in various shapes and sizes and are great for creating leaves and florals on cookies (see pages 73 and 107). However, cleaning them took a lot of work, and I found the tips clogged easily.

I was extremely pleased when I discovered tipless piping bags, which are used to outline, flood, and pipe details. These thin, disposable, lightweight bags don't require tips and help reduce hand fatigue when piping for long periods of time. The seam on the bag is small and doesn't get in the way while decorating. I'll show you how to fill and use both.

## FILLING A TIPPED PIPING BAG

### MATERIALS

Sharp scissors

Tipless piping bag

Piping tip

Tall glass

Spoon or silicone spatula

Sturdy bag clip

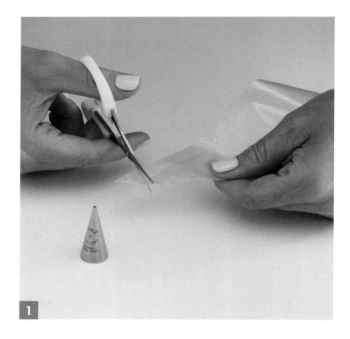

1. With sharp scissors, cut straight across the tip of the bag, just enough so the opening of the bag covers half of the piping tip (the diameter of the hole should be approximately ½" [1.3 cm] wide). Slide the piping tip into the hole.

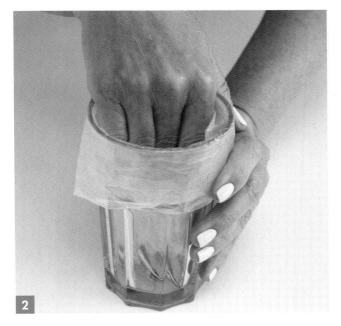

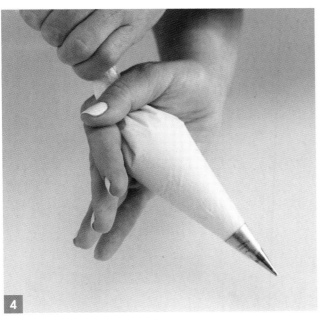

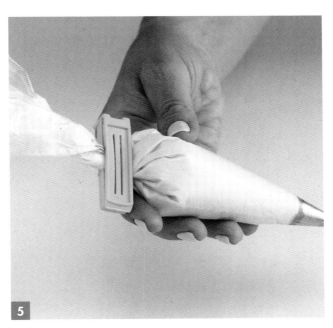

2. Place the bag inside the glass, with the tip facing down, and pull the end of the bag over the edges of the glass. Open the bag inside in the cup. There should be a large opening to spoon in the icing.

3. Transfer the icing from the bowl to the bag with a spoon or silicone spatula.

4. Pull the piping bag out of the cup. Squeeze the icing toward the piping tip while gripping the top of the bag.

5. Twist the bag just above the icing and secure it with a sturdy clip or tie the bag in a secure knot.

# FILLING A TIPLESS PIPING BAG

## MATERIALS

Tipless piping bag

Sharp scissors

Tall glass

Spoon or silicone spatula

Sturdy bag clip

1. Follow steps 2 through 5 on the previous page for filling a tipped piping bag (see page 48).

2. Cut the tip straight across with scissors. Cut about ⅛" (4 mm) from the end of the bag. The hole size should be similar to a #2 piping tip (see page 26). You can always make the hole larger if it's not wide enough to provide a smooth flow of icing.

3. Gently pinch the tip to open the hole. The piping bag is now ready to use.

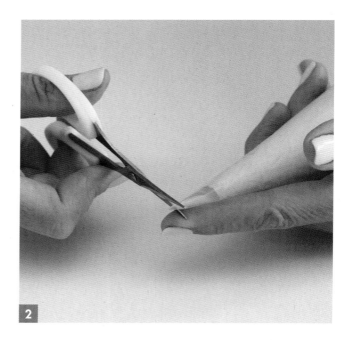

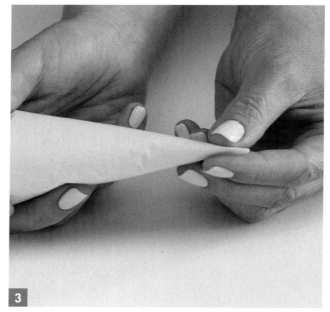

## FILLING PIPING BAGS WITHOUT A GLASS

### MATERIALS

Tipless piping bag with or without a piping tip

Silicone spatula

Sturdy bag clip

1. Choose whether you will use a piping tip (see page 48) or not (see opposite) and prepare the piping bag accordingly.

2. Hold the piping bag with your nondominant hand and fold the top of the bag down with your other hand to form a cuff.

3. With a silicone spatula, fill the bag about half to three-quarters with icing, leaving room at the top.

4. As you remove the spatula from the bag, squeeze the sides of the bag around the spatula to scrape off the excess icing.

5. Unfold the cuff and twist the bag closed. This will help push the icing down toward the tip. Close the bag with a clip or tie a knot. Cut off the tip, if necessary (see opposite).

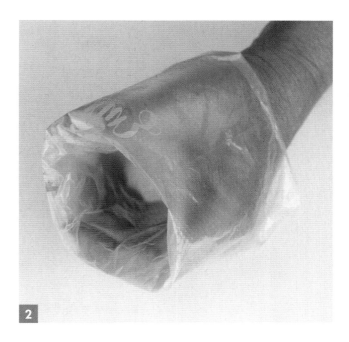

# ICING COOKIES

As mentioned previously, I prefer to use one consistency for outlining and flooding designs. I'll explain the methods of using one consistency versus two consistencies. And I'll show you my favorite way to hold a piping bag, but there's no right or wrong way to do this. If you don't find the method comfortable, try different positions to see what works best for you.

When using two icing consistencies, it's a good idea to use piping consistency to outline shapes and create straight lines and sharp, pointed corners. Use medium consistency to outline any shape that flows or arches, such as circles, scalloped edges, and plaques. The icing flows more easily out of the bag, allowing for smoother piping. If the icing is too thick, you won't get that smooth flow.

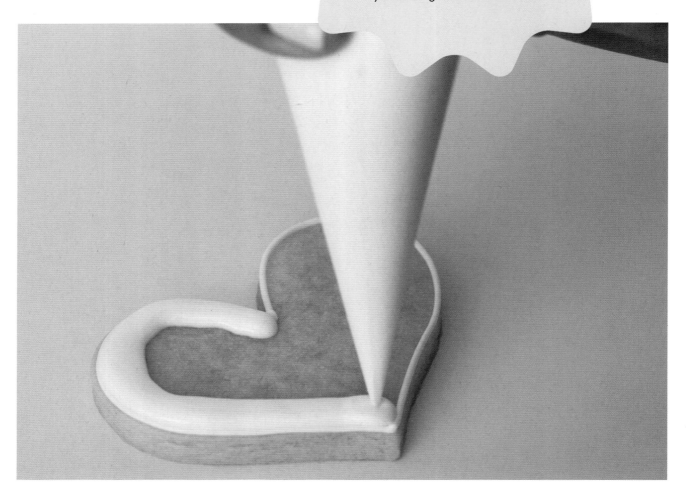

## Outline and Flood: Using Two Icing Consistencies

I recommended using this two-consistency method for outlining and flooding cookies 3" (7.5 cm) or larger. But thin icing can spill off the edges of the cookie, so you'll need to pipe the border first, allow it to harden for about 1 minute, then fill the cookie with flood-consistency icing. I also prefer this method when I'm flooding designs with sharp edges, such as hexagons, squares, or stars, since piping-consistency icing holds its shape on corners.

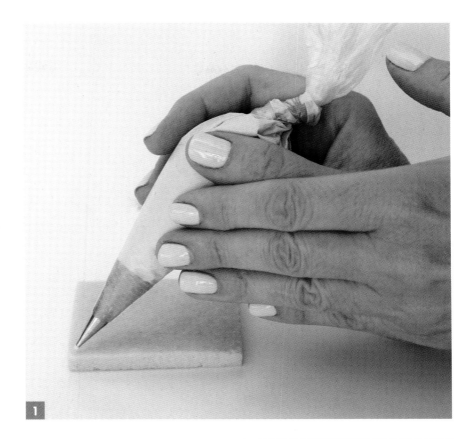

1. Fill a tipless bag with piping-consistency icing and use a #2 tip (see page 26). Grip the bag with your dominant hand and place the twisted part between your thumb and forefinger. Place one or two fingers of your other hand on the bag to keep it steady. Place the piping tip on the edge of the cookie, holding the bag at a 45-degree angle.

2. Gently squeeze the bag while pulling it slightly upward over the cookie. I like to hover around ½" (1.3 cm) above the cookie surface.

*(continued)*

3. Allow the icing to flow smoothly out of the bag onto the cookie, keeping even pressure on the bag. This allows for a smooth flow of icing that falls perfectly into place.

4. When working with shapes that have corners, let the tip of the bag touch the cookie at each corner, rather than continue to pipe in one steady movement. This makes the corners sharp. Rotate the cookie and continue to pipe the remaining sides. Allow the completed border to set for about 1 minute.

5. Fit another piping bag with a #3 tip (see page 26) and fill with flood-consistency icing. To flood the cookie, start in one corner and use steady pressure to squeeze out the icing throughout this step.

Use the flat edge of a 2-in-1 tool (boo-boo stick) to scrape any icing mistakes off your cookie.

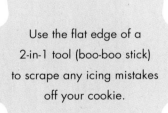

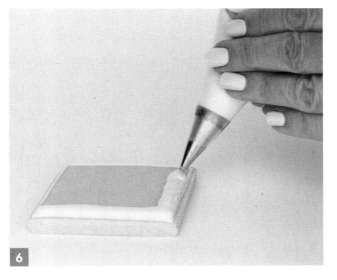

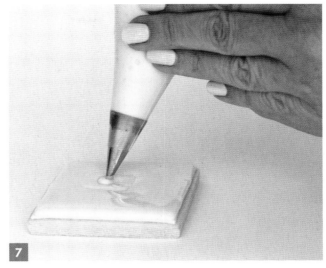

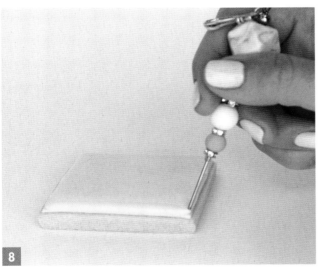

6. Flood the perimeter of the area first, staying tight against the piped border.

7. Continue flooding the cookie at a steady pace, since the icing begins to set quickly. Add icing until you get to the center of the cookie.

8. Use the scribe tool to move the icing around and fill in any small gaps, smooth the icing, or pop air bubbles.

9. The result is a beautifully iced cookie with crisp edges. Once the cookie is iced, place the finished cookie in front of a fan (see page 27) to begin the drying process for about 30 minutes, then turn off the fan and allow it to dry completely, 8 to 12 hours or overnight.

If the cookie surface needs to be further smoothed after scribing, give it a gentle shake. Be careful not to touch the icing surface.

## Outline and Flood: Using One Icing Consistency

This is my preferred method for outlining and flooding smaller cookies that uses a slightly thicker consistency of flood icing and one piping bag. This is not ideal for cookies larger than 3". Because the icing is thicker, it won't ooze off the sides, but will leave a puffy seamless outline. It also saves time and there's less to clean up.

1. Fill a tipless piping bag with medium-consistency icing and snip the top off the bag with sharp scissors (see page 50). Determine where you want to start piping the outline, and gently squeeze the bag. Continue squeezing the piping bag using steady pressure while outlining the shape, hovering just above the cookie surface.

2. Immediately after the outline is complete, begin to flood the cookie, using the same piping bag and starting right next to the outline. Use increased pressure on the bag as you flood the area.

3. Continue piping in a circular motion, making sure there are no gaps in the icing as you go.

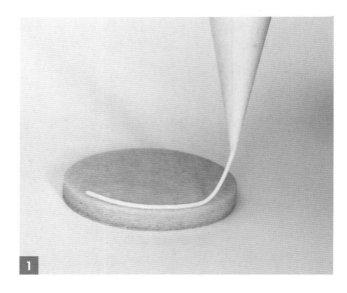

**4.** At the center of the cookie, release pressure on the bag and pull it straight up and away from the cookie.

**5.** Use the scribe tool to redistribute the icing or move it around to fill in any gaps. If the icing hasn't settled on its own, give the cookie a gentle shake, making sure not to damage the surface.

**6.** You should have a perfectly iced cookie that looks slightly puffed. Place the finished cookie in front of a fan (see page 27) to begin the drying process for about 30 minutes, then turn off the fan and allow it to dry completely, 8 to 12 hours or overnight.

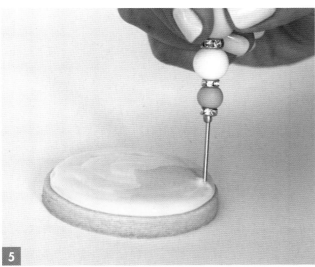

## CONSISTENCY WITH CONSISTENCIES

I typically use one consistency of royal icing when decorating cookies, and each cookie project in this book includes the recommended consistency. The icing may be thicker than you're comfortable working with, or you may prefer to use different consistencies for outlining and flooding (or filling) designs. Feel free to use two consistencies at any time—a thicker one to outline and a thinner one to flood. There is no right or wrong method, so do what works best for you.

I also recommend using a tabletop fan to dry freshly iced cookies. Note that the cookies don't need to be in front of a fan during the entire drying time. A general rule is to begin the drying process by placing the cookies in front of a fan for 30 minutes, which allows the icing to set. Turn the fan off and allow the cookies to dry fully as per the times indicated in the recipe. The cookies should remain uncovered during the drying process.

# WET-ON-WET ICING TECHNIQUE

The wet-on-wet technique is one of the first ones I experimented with in my early days of cookie decorating. I like this method because you can achieve beautiful intricate designs with minimal effort.

The technique involves piping flood-consistency royal icing on top of flood-consistency royal icing while the first layer is still wet. Working quickly is essential. Make sure all the colors are mixed and the piping bags are filled. If you're using tipless bags, cut all the tips so they're ready to go. I like to line up my piping bags in the order I'll be piping them, so I can grab and pipe.

I prefer using two consistencies for this technique: piping- or medium-consistency icing for the outline (see pages 46 to 47) and flood-consistency icing to fill the cookie and create designs. Once you begin piping designs on the wet base, the icing may spill off the sides of the cookie if the border hasn't slightly crusted over.

Plan your design in advance and sketch it on paper so you can pipe quickly. I created a leaf motif, which is easy to do freehand. If you take more than 45 to 60 seconds to create the design, the icing will begin to harden and you won't achieve a smooth surface. You can practice on a piece of parchment paper first. Keep in mind that weather conditions, such as heat and humidity, can impact how quickly the icing will set.

## MATERIALS

Baked and cooled hexagon-shaped cookies

Tipless piping bags

Piping-consistency royal icing, white (see page 46)

Flood-consistency royal icing, white, dark green, and light green (see page 47)

Scribe tool

Edible ink pen, black, fine tip

Dusting brush and cornstarch (optional)

1. Outline the cookie using piping-consistency icing in white (see page 56). Allow it to set for about 1 minute.

2. Use flood-consistency icing in white to fill the cookie (see pages 56 to 57). For the following steps, work quickly while the base is freshly iced.

3. Pipe leaf patterns with the dark green icing. Simple designs are best for wet-on-wet techniques, since the technique isn't suited for complex shapes. Being precise is difficult when you're using flood-consistency icing and working quickly.

*(continued)*

4. Drag the scribe tool from the center of each leaf to the tip to emphasize the leaf shape.

5. Pipe accent leaves with the light green icing and allow it to fully dry overnight.

6. Outline the designs using the edible ink pen.

7. If you plan to package the cookies, wait until the ink is fully dry (this may take an hour or more), and dust the cookies with cornstarch and a large dusting brush prior to wrapping them. The cornstarch will absorb any moisture from the edible ink pen.

# ROYAL ICING TRANSFERS

Royal icing transfers are edible sugar decorations that are piped onto wax paper, parchment paper, or food-safe acetate sheets, then transferred to cookies. To make the process easier and more efficient I print out designs on a piece of paper, then place it under the clear or translucent transfer sheet so it can act as a template.

After the royal icing designs are piped and fully dry, peel them off and adhere them to the cookies using royal icing as glue.

A template is needed for this technique. Designs can be purchased online, or you can find copyright-free motifs. You can also draw your own patterns and scan them or use a digital design program. I recommend using simple designs and shapes and one color when starting out. Once the template is printed and placed underneath the transfer sheet, tape the corners of the transfer sheet so it doesn't move while you're piping.

Royal icing transfers can help save time on projects. They can be prepared days or weeks in advance and stored in an airtight container until ready to use.

## MATERIALS

Printed template

Wax paper, parchment paper, or food-safe acetate sheet

Tape

Tipless piping bag

Medium-consistency royal icing, any color (see page 47)

Scribe tool

*(continued)*

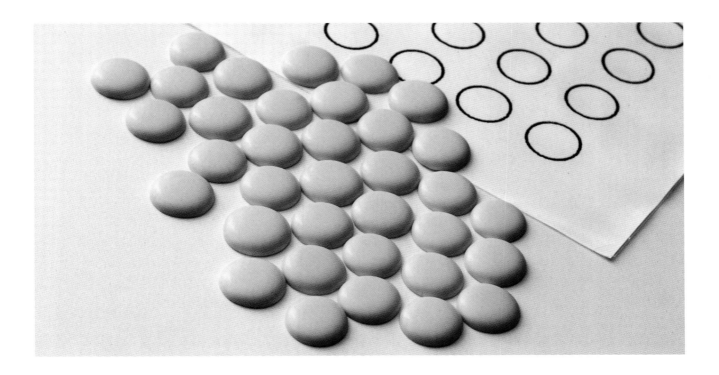

1. Place the template underneath the wax paper and tape the edges of the sheet so it doesn't move while you're piping. Prepare and fill a tipless piping bag (see page 50). Outline the design with the icing (see page 56). Flood the center of the design using the same icing (see page 57).

2. Pipe a generous amount of icing in the center of the circle. This will help prevent the center from sinking or dipping, as it's called in the cookie world, and create a puffy look. Use the scribe tool to smooth the icing if needed.

3. Allow the icing transfers to fully dry for at least 24 hours uncovered. I usually place the transfers in front of a tabletop fan immediately after piping them for 1 to 2 hours. This will help prevent the icing from dipping and forming craters, and will also create a sheen on the icing.

4. Gently peel the transfers off of the sheet (sometimes they'll pop off). If the pieces are stuck, they're not fully dry and may break if you attempt to peel them off. Continue to let them dry until they can be removed easily.

5. The transfers are ready to use. To adhere them to cookies, apply them directly to freshly flooded icing, or apply a small amount of royal icing to the back of the transfer to glue it in place.

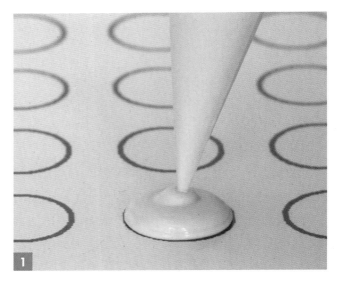

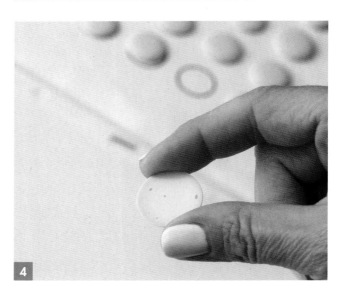

# BASKETWEAVE

This fun technique creates the look of a woven basket that can be paired with flowers, greenery, and other designs. After a bit of practice, you'll be able to recreate this look with ease. You'll incorporate this motif to create a floral basket (see page 107). As a bonus, the technique can also be used on cakes.

## MATERIALS

Piping bags

Basketweave piping tip #47

Stiff-consistency royal icing, light brown (see page 46)

Parchment or wax paper

Tape

Baked and cooled cookies

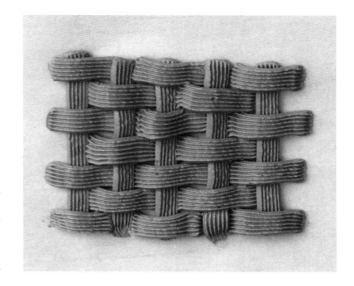

1. Fit a piping bag with the basketweave tip and fill with stiff-consistency royal icing (see page 46). I used brown icing, but you can use any color. Place a piece of parchment or wax paper on a flat surface and tape it down if necessary so it doesn't move while you work. Hold the piping tip flat on the surface with the serrated side facing up.

*(continued)*

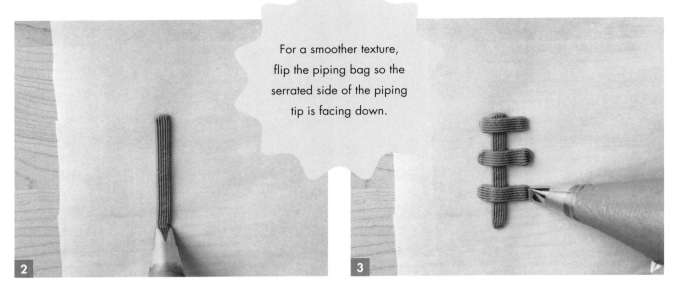

For a smoother texture, flip the piping bag so the serrated side of the piping tip is facing down.

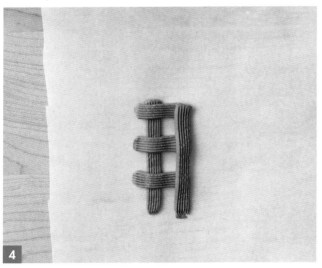

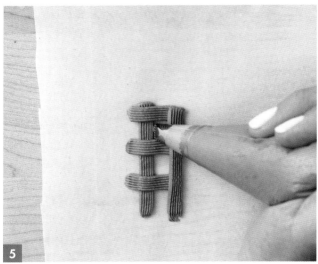

**2.** With steady pressure, pipe a vertical stripe about 3" (7.5 cm) long. To create a clean edge, press the tip onto the paper when finished piping the stripe. Be sure to maintain steady pressure while piping with stiff icing, otherwise the icing can break mid-flow. If this happens, continue from the break, or use the 2-in-1 tool to lift and pull away the icing that broke.

**3.** Pipe three ¾" (2 cm)-wide horizontal stripes across the vertical stripe, starting just below the top. The gap between each stripe should be the same width as the piping tip. Pipe a dot between each stripe to help gauge the spacing.

**4.** Pipe another vertical stripe just over the ends of the horizontal stripes, again using steady pressure on the piping bag.

**5.** Start the next row of horizontal stripes by placing the piping tip flush against the right edge of the first vertical stripe.

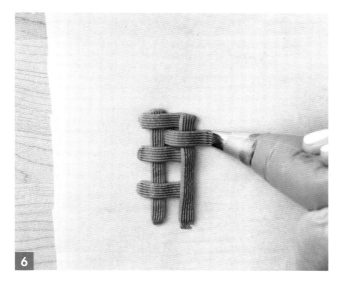

**6.** Pipe a horizontal stripe across the vertical one, as you did before, but staggering them in the spaces made in the first stripe.

**7.** Continue to make horizontal stripes.

**8.** Repeat steps 4 to 6 to make another vertical stripe and another row of horizontal stripes. Repeat the pattern until you have created the basket size you need.

# HAND PAINTING

Hand painting is my favorite way to decorate cookies. I fell in love with the technique after I painted my first princess character. This method allows you to create a simple watercolor effect or a fine-detailed portrait using liquid gel or gel food paste and water. Many people find the technique to be therapeutic, and for basic designs like this one no special artistic skills are required. Always start with a white icing background.

## MATERIALS

Baked and iced cookies in a flower and leaf design (see opposite)

Medium- and flood-consistency icing royal icing, white (see page 47)

Edible ink pen, light brown, fine tip

Assorted food-safe paintbrushes (I used round brushes, sizes 3 to 7)

Bowl of water

Paper towels

Liquid gel or gel food coloring in forest green, burgundy, golden yellow, leaf green, fuchsia, brown, and white

Paint palette

1. Prepare a batch of iced cookies at least 24 hours before decorating to allow the icing to fully set. Outline in medium and fill with white flood-consistency royal icing (see page 56). This will ensure the icing doesn't flow off into the crevices of this shape.

2. Draw an outline of the flower and leaves on the icing using a light brown edible food pen, following the shape of the cookie. The outline is meant as a guide—it doesn't have to be perfect, since you'll paint over it. If you feel confident in your painting skills, you can omit this step.

3. Dip a size 3 round paintbrush in water and blot off the excess moisture on a paper towel. Blotting off the excess water on the paintbrush is essential. If there's too much water on the brush, it can cause pooling on the surface of the cookie and damage the icing.

   Add a single drop of forest green gel food coloring to a palette well and dip the tip of the brush in it (add more colorant if it runs out). Holding the brush almost parallel to the paper towel, blot off the excess gel.

   Hold the brush at a slight angle and paint the outline of all the leaves.

*(continued)*

A llight brown, fine tip, edible ink pen is recommended for drawing the outline because it blends in easily with the paint. Dark colors, such as black or red, can alter the color of the gel and stain the cookie base.

4. Clean the brush by swirling it in water until no color is left in the bristles. Dab the excess water on a paper towel. Note: If the water becomes dirty, refill the bowl with fresh water. Drag the brush from the leaf outline inward, pulling the color toward the center to fill in the leaves.

5. Repeat steps 2 through 4 to outline and fill in the flower petals, using burgundy gel.

6. Paint the middle of the flower using golden yellow, using the same technique. Move the brush in a circular motion to pull the color inward from the outline. Paint the inner edges of the leaf outlines with leaf green, using a back-and-forth motion to blend the color. Brush golden yellow in the middle of the leaves, blending it the same way.

7. Add dimension to the petals by brushing fuchsia gel from the base of the petal outward. Blend the color so it looks smooth, not streaky.

8. Dip a fine-tipped brush into brown gel. Gently blot the brush on the paper towel so it's not oversaturated with the gel and touch the tip of the brush in the center of the flower to create tiny dots.

9. With the same brush and brown gel, paint the stem and outline some sections of the leaves. I added outlines in random spots to add detail to the leaves.

10. Create highlights on the flowers by brushing white gel coloring in the center of the petals. Be sure to blend the color well so it appears smooth.

11. Blend white gel coloring in the center of the leaves to add additional highlights.

Hand-painted cookies are usually dry and ready to package within a few hours of finishing them. However, they may take longer to dry. If packaging the cookies in cellophane bags, gently dust the surface of the cookie with cornstarch using a large, soft, food-safe brush.

# BRUSHED EMBROIDERY

Although this embroidery technique may look difficult, it's one of the simpler designs to create. These floral motifs are perfect for themes that call for elegance and class. Use gentle brushstrokes with the paintbrush and use your imagination to create unique floral shapes.

A scribe tool can be used to lightly etch floral shapes in the royal icing before piping. This can help you plan the layout of the design. Once you etch into a cookie you cannot remove the scratch marks. However, you can change the design and pipe over the marks to hide them.

## MATERIALS

Baked and iced cookies (see opposite)

Piping- and flood-consistency royal icing, blue (see pages 46 to 47)

Piping bag

Round piping tip #2 or a tipless piping bag (see page 48)

Piping-consistency royal icing, white (see page 46)

Flat paintbrush, size 5

Small bowl of water

Paper towels

Scribe tool

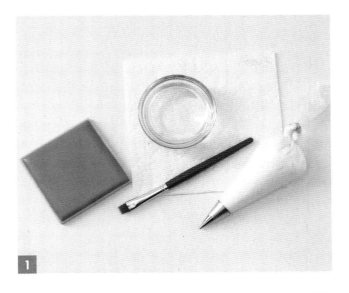

1. Prepare a batch of iced cookies at least 12 hours before decorating. Outline the cookies with piping-consistency royal icing and flood them with flood-consistency icing (see page 47). I usually ice the cookies the night before decorating them and allow the icing to fully set. I used a color by Roxy & Rich called Wedgewood (one of my favorite shades), but feel free to use any color you like. Be sure to have all the tools and supplies ready before starting; the piped icing must be wet while working with it.

2. Fit a piping bag with the #2 round tip and fill with white piping-consistency royal icing (see page 48).

3. Pipe a wavy flower petal outline using a zigzag motion, keeping the piping tip angled at 45 degrees. Begin piping anywhere on the cookie.

4. Immediately dip the brush in water and blot it on the paper towel to remove excess moisture. Be sure to blot both sides of the brush.

*(continued)*

When blotting the brush, make sure that the bristles are flat on the paper towel. Blotting the brush by tapping it down on the paper towel can damage the bristles.

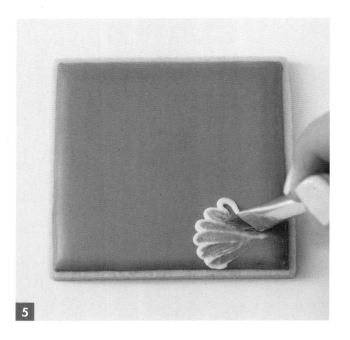

**5.** Brush the icing from the inside edge inward using the tip of the bristles, not the flat part, and holding the brush at a 45-degree angle. Work quickly while the icing is still wet.

**6.** Repeat steps 3 through 5 to create more petals and leaf shapes. Layer and group elements to create dimension. Let your imagination guide you.

**7.** When you feel you've added enough motifs, your beautiful cookies are complete. Allow the icing to dry for at least an hour before handling them.

# ROYAL ICING FLOWERS

These beautiful icing flowers can be used as simple accents or to create a blooming garden on your cookies. Make gorgeous, eye-catching flowers in different sizes and shapes using a variety of piping tips. If stored properly, the flowers can be prepared in advance and used later.

## Star Flower

I use these small star shapes as fillers in my royal icing flower gardens.

### MATERIALS

Tipless piping bags

Open star piping tip, #14, #16, or #18 (depending on the size you prefer)

Stiff-consistency royal icing, any color (see page 46)

Parchment or wax paper taped to a flat surface, such as a cookie sheet or pan

*(continued)*

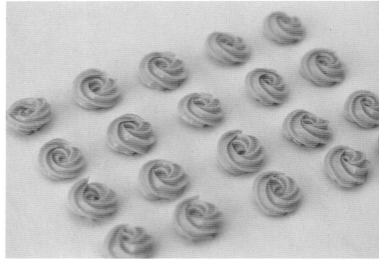

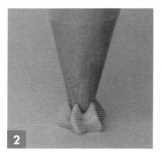

1. Fit a piping bag with the open star tip and fill with stiff-consistency royal icing (see page 46). Hold the bag straight up over the wax paper with the tip approximately ⅛" (3 mm) above the surface.

2. Squeeze icing onto the sheet to form a star.

3. Release the pressure on the piping bag, then pull it away.

## Rosette

These florals, also known as rose swirls, are my favorite royal icing flowers. They're quick and easy to make.

### MATERIALS

Tipless piping bags

Open star piping tip, #16 or #18 (depending on the size you prefer)

Stiff-consistency royal icing, any color (see page 46)

Parchment or wax paper taped to a flat surface, such as a cookie sheet or pan

2-in-1 tool

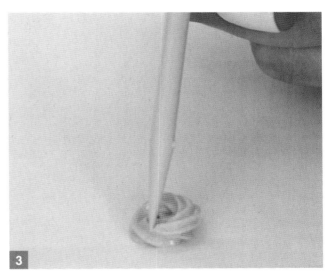

1. Fit a piping bag with the piping tip and fill with stiff-consistency royal icing (see page 46). Hold the bag straight up over the parchment paper with the piping tip approximately 1⅛" (3 mm) above the surface. Squeeze the piping bag to form a star.

2. Raise the tip slightly while keeping pressure on the bag and allow the icing to flow as you continue to swirl the icing around the star, using one continuous motion (2A). Move clockwise around the star (if you're left-handed, you may want to move counterclockwise), beginning at 9:00, moving to 12:00, 3:00, and 6:00. When you reach the 6:00 point, release pressure from the bag while continuing to rotate the bag slightly, going back to the starting point at 9:00. Slowly pull the tip away, still traveling clockwise (2B).

3. Use the 2-in-1 tool to gently press down any icing that may not have settled.

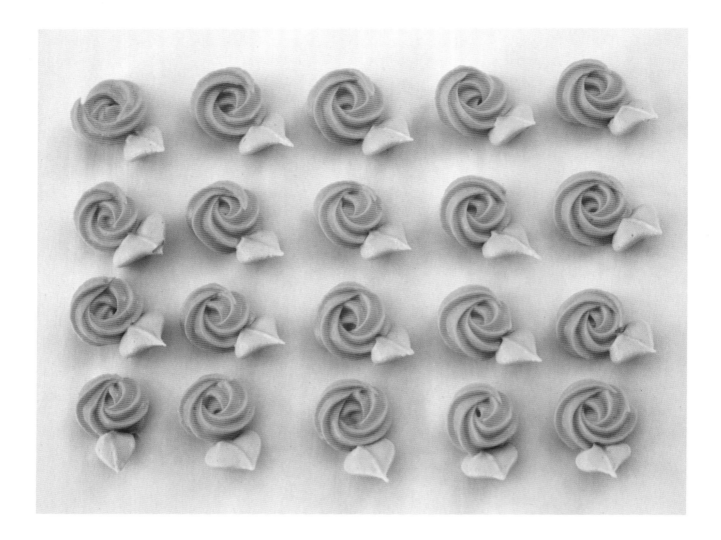

## Leaves

Making leaves is almost effortless when you use a leaf tip. Create a basic or ruffled shape simply by changing the way you squeeze the piping bag.

**MATERIALS**

Piping bag

Leaf piping tip (I used Wilton #352)

Stiff-consistency royal icing, light green (see page 46)

Piped rosettes on parchment or wax paper (see page 74)

1. For this technique you'll pipe leaves next to premade rosette flowers. Fit a piping bag with the leaf piping tip and fill with stiff-consistency royal icing (see page 46). To form a basic leaf, hold the bag at 45 degrees, with the tip just slightly touching the surface of the parchment paper next to the rosette.

2. Squeeze the bag firmly while holding it in position and create a substantial base for the leaf.

3. Create the leaf by slowly raising the tip away from the surface, gradually releasing pressure on the piping bag. Stop squeezing the bag as you pull the tip away, forming the leaf point. Repeat, making as many leaves as you need.

4. To form a ruffled leaf, move the tip in a quick back-and-forth motion as you pipe it.

# Apple Blossoms

This flower is perfect for tropical-themed cookies.

## MATERIALS

Tipless piping bags

Petal piping tip (I used Wilton #102)

Stiff-consistency royal icing, any color
(see page 46)

Flower nail (can be made of metal or plastic,
available at baking supply and some craft stores)

Parchment paper cut into 1½" (4 cm) squares

Medium-consistency royal icing, yellow
(see page 47)

1.  Fit a piping bag with a petal piping tip and fill with
    stiff-consistency royal icing (see page 48). Hold the
    piping bag in your dominant hand and the flower nail
    in the other hand. Squeeze a small amount of royal
    icing onto the center of the flower nail and use it to
    adhere a piece of parchment paper.

2.  For this five-petal flower, you'll pipe one petal at a
    time. Hold the piping bag at a 45-degree angle with
    the wide end lightly touching the center of the nail.
    The narrow end of the tip should be pointing out
    while slightly angled above the surface.

3.  Squeeze the bag and create an arc motion while
    turning the flower nail.

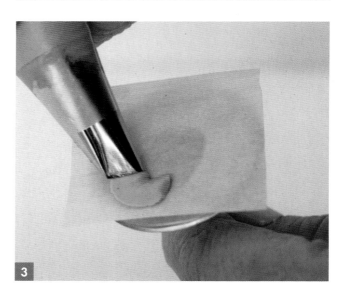

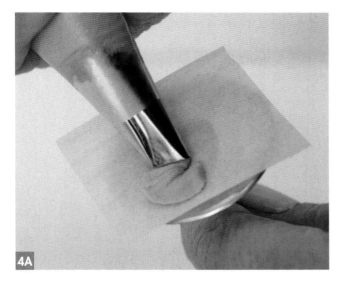

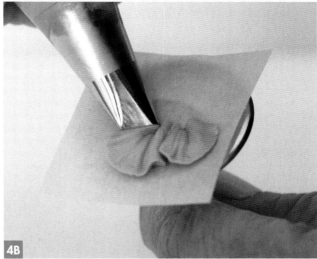

4. Release the pressure on the bag as you return to the starting point (4A). The slight ruffling in the petals should happen naturally as you pipe (4B).

5. Repeat steps 3 and 4 to create four more petals.

6. Prepare a tipless piping bag with medium-consistency yellow royal icing (see page 48). Cut the tip of the piping bag about ⅛" (3 mm) from the tip. Pipe five small dots in the center of the flower.

7. Carefully slide the parchment paper off the nail and place it on a flat surface to dry overnight. When the flowers are completely dry, they should pop off the parchment.

## Large Swirl Flower

I'm not sure whether this flower has a formal name in the cookie world, but I call it a large swirl flower. This floral, which is larger than the rosette (see page 74) and apple blossom (see page 78), adds a whimsical look to your royal icing garden.

### MATERIALS

| |
|---|
| Piping bags |
| Petal piping tip (I used Wilton #104) |
| Stiff-consistency royal icing, any color (see page 46) |
| Flower nail |
| Parchment paper cut into 1½" (4 cm) squares |
| 2-in-1 tool |

1. Fit a piping bag with the petal piping tip and fill with stiff-consistency royal icing (see page 48). Squeeze a small amount of royal icing onto the center of the flower nail and press a small square piece of parchment paper onto the icing.

2. As with the apple blossom, hold the piping bag at a 45-degree angle with the wide end lightly touching the center of the nail. The narrow end of the tip should be pointing out while slightly angled above the surface. Starting on the outside of the flower nail, squeeze the bag while rotating the nail.

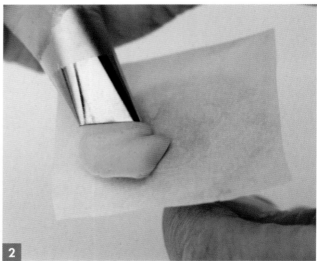

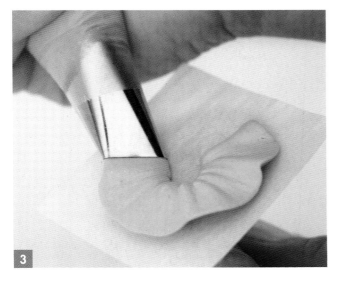

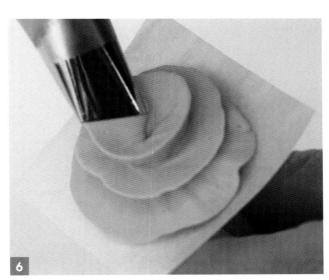

3. Continue to squeeze the bag and rotate the flower nail as you create a border around the nail, using consistent pressure throughout the entire movement. Wiggle the piping bag a little as you pipe to achieve a ruffled effect. This flower is created with one continuous spiral instead of separate petals.

4. While continuing to rotate the flower nail, pipe another petal layer on the inside of the border.

5. Continue piping, creating another layer as you move closer to the center.

6. Release pressure on the piping bag as you reach the center, then lift the piping tip and pull the bag away. Use a 2-in-1 tool to push down any icing that might have lifted up in the center of the flower. Slide the parchment paper off the flower nail and place the completed flower on a flat surface to dry overnight.

# FONDANT ACCENTS WITH SILICONE MOLDS

Molds made from food-grade silicone allow you to create detailed shapes to accent your cookie designs. They can be used with chocolate, gum paste (edible, moldable sugar dough), isomalt (a sugar substitute typically used for decoration), candy, and more. I'll show you how to get stunning results using fondant.

You can make fondant from scratch or use ready-made (which I often do). Pre-colored, ready-made fondant can be found in specialty stores and some craft stores, or you can use white fondant and color it yourself. Dust or powder colorants or gel food colorants work best. Liquid colorants can make the fondant become sticky. If this happens, add some powdered sugar to the fondant until you reach the desired consistency again.

## MATERIALS

Food-safe silicone mold

Cornstarch

Large food-safe brush

Fondant, white or any color (the amount will depend on how many molds you plan to make)

Dust or gel colorant, any color

Food-safe protective gloves

Mini scoop about ¼" (6 mm) wide

Parchment paper

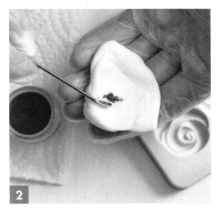

1. Dust the mold with cornstarch, using a large brush. This helps prevent the fondant from sticking to the mold.

2. Color the fondant. I used dust colorant (see page 38), but you can also use gel food paste or liquid gel. Wearing food-safe gloves and using a mini scoop, scoop a small amount of dust into the center of the fondant. Fold the fondant to encase the colorant. If you're using pre-colored fondant, skip this step.

3. Stretch and twist the fondant until the color is fully combined. Add more colorant if needed until you reach the desired shade.

4. Roll the fondant into balls and let it sit for a few minutes to firm up slightly before pressing it into the molds.

5. Press the fondant into the mold cavities, making sure the fondant is flush with the top of the mold. Place the mold in the refrigerator for a few minutes or leave it on the counter until the fondant firms up.

6. Carefully pop the fondant pieces out of the mold and place them on a piece of parchment paper until ready to use. To adhere fondant accents to cookies, pipe a small amount of medium-consistency royal icing on the back of the fondant piece and gently press it into place.

# 3

# SEASONAL COOKIES

Practice the art of cookie decorating all year long with the incredible seasonal cookie designs in this chapter. Incorporate the techniques you've learned and make a festive hat, mitten, snowflake, and a snowy tree for winter. Welcome spring with an adorable bird, various types of flowers, a carrot, and a flower-crowned bunny. Jump into summer and create a surfboard, Hawaiian shirt, flip-flops, a bathing suit, a beach scene with shells, and a vibrant starfish. And celebrate fall with a rustic wreath, leafy branch, a brilliant sunflower, colorful sugar skull, and a not-so-scary ghost. You'll never lack ideas or inspiration with these projects, which will be the main attraction of any gathering.

# WINTER COOKIES

# SNOWFLAKE

This snowflake will glisten on your platter, just as it does when it falls from the sky and settles on the ground. Take these cookies from basic to blingy by adding edible glitter to the surface!

## MATERIALS

Baked and cooled snowflake-shaped cookies

Tipless piping bags

Piping-consistency royal icing, white (see page 46)

Flood-consistency royal icing, white (see page 47)

Edible glitter, white, in a pump bottle (see page 30) (I used Roxy & Rich Satin White Sparkle Dust)

Scribe tool

Silver dragées

Rubber-tipped tweezers

**Note:** For this cookie, you'll use piping-consistency royal icing for the outline and flood-consistency icing to cover the surface. The multiple angles of the cutter dictate this choice; if you were to use flood-consistency icing to outline the cookie, it would likely spill over the edges.

1.  Fill a tipless piping bag with piping-consistency white royal icing (see page 50). Outline the cookie with the icing (see page 53). Since this shape has so many angles, hold the piping bag close to the cookie, about ½" (1.3 cm) away from the surface, which allows you to have more control over the piping. Begin piping slowly from any of the outer points, slowing down the motion as you come to the inner points.

Allow the piping tip to touch the inner corners of the cookie, then slowly pull the piping bag up as you repeat this process for each angle. Allow the icing to set for about 30 seconds before going on to the next step.

2. Fill a tipless piping bag with flood-consistency white royal icing (see page 49). Fill each pointed section one at a time, then fill the center. Place the cookie in front of a tabletop fan for about 10 minutes or until the icing just starts to crust over before moving on to the next step.

3. Handle the cookie gently if you need to move it. Spray edible glitter onto the surface of the icing. Applying it at this stage, while the icing is still tacky, allows for better adhesion. Allow the cookie to continue to dry for 8 to 12 hours, or overnight.

4. Using piping-consistency icing, pipe a line of icing from one arm of the snowflake to the other.

5. Pipe two more similar lines across the cookie.

*(continued)*

6. Use the piped lines to create six V-shaped lines near the center of the cookie.

7. Pipe the same V-shaped lines near the tips of the snowflakes.

8. Pipe a small dot on the tips of the snowflakes, slightly dragging the piping bag toward the center of the cookie to create a teardrop shape. Or pipe a dot and use the scribe tool to drag the icing to create a teardrop shape.

9. Pipe a small dot of icing in the center of the cookie. While the icing is still wet, adhere a silver dragée, using rubber-tipped tweezers. Gently push the dragée into the icing. The icing should be fully dry in 2 hours.

I like using rubber-tipped tweezers to pick up sugar pearls and sprinkles, as they're less likely to slip away.

# KNITTED MITTENS AND POM-POM HAT

You don't have to know how to knit to make these adorable mittens and hat. The key to creating the knitted look is being consistent with the small piped dots that form the stitches. A little practice will help ensure a clean, professional look.

## MATERIALS

Tipless piping bags

Medium-consistency royal icing, light blue (see page 47)

Flood-consistency royal icing, light blue (see page 47)

Piping tip #2 (optional; beginners may find it easier to create the knit pattern using a piping tip)

**For the mittens:**

Baked and cooled mitten-shaped cookies

Brown fondant

Food-safe button mold

**For the hat:**

Baked and cooled winter hat–shaped cookies

Medium-consistency royal icing, white (see page 47)

White nonpareils

*(continued)*

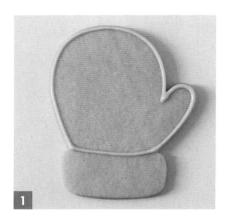

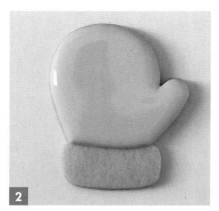

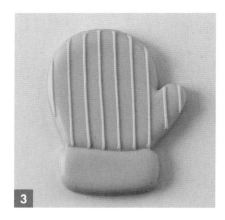

## Mittens

1. Fill a tipless piping bag with medium-consistency light blue royal icing (see page 48). Outline the mitten.

2. Fill a tipless piping bag with light blue flood-consistency royal icing. Cover the cookie surface with the icing and place it in front of a tabletop fan to dry for at least 3 hours. The icing doesn't need to be completely dry before adding the piped details, since they're lightweight. However, be careful handling the cookies while decorating them because you can damage the icing.

3. Pipe a series of vertical lines on the top portion of the mitten with medium-consistency icing, leaving an equal amount of space between the lines. Outline and flood the cuff. Place the cookie in front of a tabletop fan to dry for at least another 3 hours.

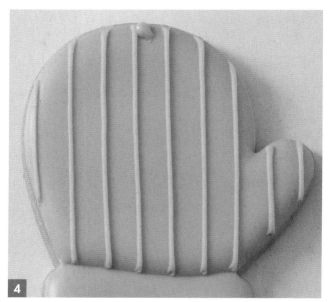

4. Begin creating the stitch pattern within the center lines. If you prefer, fit the piping bag with the piping tip. Using medium-consistency icing, pipe a small dot in the top left section within the center lines. Release pressure on the piping bag as you drag the icing slightly downward and toward the right.

5. Repeat step 4, piping adjacent to where you just piped the previous dot. This time, drag the icing downward and toward the left.

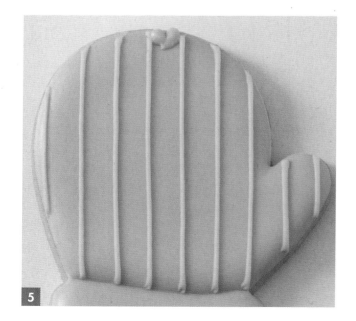

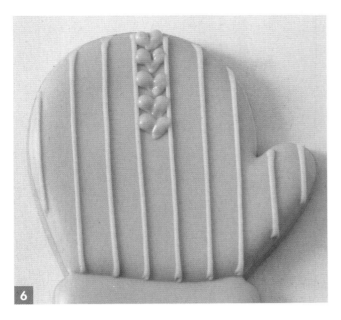

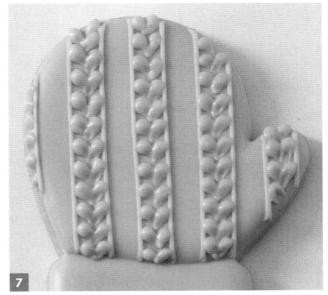

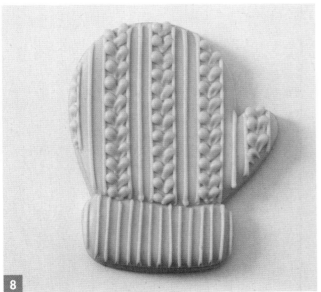

6. Continue this pattern all the way down between the center lines.

7. Repeat the knit pattern within every other set of lines.

8. Pipe an additional vertical line between the knitted stitches using medium-consistency icing. Use the same icing to pipe vertical lines on the cuff, starting in the middle and working outward and spacing the lines equally.

9. Create a brown fondant button, using a mold (see page 82). Squeeze a small amount of medium-consistency icing on the back of the button and use light pressure to set it in place. Allow the cookie to dry for 8 to 12 hours, or overnight, prior to packaging.

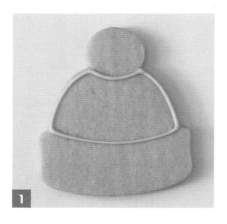

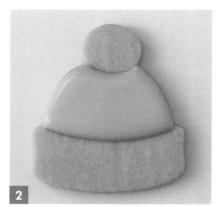

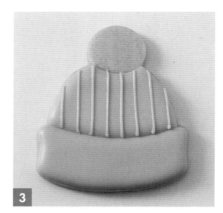

## Pom-Pom Hat

1. Fill a tipless piping bag with medium-consistency light blue royal icing (see page 48). Outline the main portion of the hat.

2. Fill a tipless piping bag with light blue flood-consistency royal icing. Fill in the outline with the icing and place it in front of a tabletop fan to dry for at least 3 hours. As with the mitten, the icing doesn't need to be completely dry before adding details, but be careful handling it.

3. Pipe a series of vertical lines on the top portion of the hat with medium-consistency icing, leaving an equal amount of space between the lines. Outline and flood the base of the hat. Place the cookie in front of a tabletop fan to dry for at least another 3 hours.

4. Create the stitch pattern and pipe additional lines on the hat and cuff following steps 4 through 8 for the mitten cookie.

5. Finish the hat by adding a pom-pom. Outline and flood the pop-pom with white medium-consistency royal icing, leaving a little space between the outline and the edge of the cookie. This helps prevent the nonpareils from spilling off the side of the cookie.

6. Sprinkle white nonpareils over the freshly iced pom-pom (see finished cookie, page 89). Allow the cookie to dry for 8 to 12 hours, or overnight, before packaging.

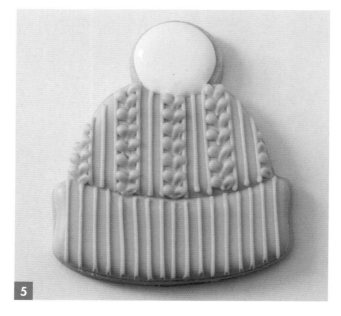

# SNOWMAN

This adorable snowman comes to life with expressive eyes, courtesy of the wet-on-wet icing technique. Brush a bit of pink luster dust on his cheeks and he's ready for a snowy day.

## MATERIALS

Baked and cooled snowman head-shaped cookies

Edible ink pens, light brown and black

Tipless piping bags

Flood-consistency royal icing, black and white (see page 47)

Medium-consistency royal icing, black, light blue, white, and orange (see page 47)

Scribe tool

Pink luster dust

Food-safe paintbrush

1. Outline the snowman's hat using a light brown edible ink pen. I prefer this color because it won't seep into the white royal icing.

*(continued)*

2. Fill tipless piping bags with medium- and flood-consistency black royal icings (see page 50). Outline the crown and brim of the hat with medium-consistency icing, but don't outline the space in between the sections, which is the hatband.

3. Fill the crown and brim with black flood-consistency icing and place it in front of a tabletop fan for about 30 minutes, or until the icing is crusted over.

4. Fill a tipless piping back with light blue medium-consistency icing and use it to outline and immediately flood the hatband. I recommend using a thicker consistency icing for small areas, since it can help prevent craters or dips from forming in the icing.

5. Fill tipless piping bags with medium- and flood-consistency white royal icings. Outline the face with medium-consistency royal icing and fill with flood-consistency icing. Allow the cookie to thoroughly dry for at least 8 hours or overnight prior to adding details.

6. It's time to make this snowman come to life! Pipe on eyebrows, using medium-consistency white royal icing. Add the eyes, using the wet-on-wet technique (see page 58). Pipe two small dots for the eyes, using black medium-consistency icing. While the icing is still wet, add smaller white dots for the eye reflections, using medium-consistency white icing.

7. Add a carrot-shaped nose. Outline the shape using orange medium-consistency icing, then flood the outline with the same icing. Create a point at the end of the nose using a scribe tool to drag the icing outward. I used an upward swooping motion to make this whimsical shape. (Trace the shape first using the light brown edible ink pen if you're not comfortable creating the design freehand.) Draw a smile on the snowman's face with a black edible ink pen.

8. Apply pink luster dust to the tip of the paintbrush and tap off the excess. Create rosy cheeks by gently swirling the brush in a circular motion. Allow the facial details to dry for at least 4 hours prior to packaging.

# SNOWY TREE

The brushed embroidery technique (see page 70) doesn't only have to be used to make frilly flower petals or lace; here it's used to create the look of snow-tipped branches on a festive tree.

## MATERIALS

Baked and cooled tree-shaped cookies

Tipless piping bags

Medium- and flood-consistency royal icing, light green (see page 47)

Stiff-consistency royal icing, white (see page 46)

Flat food-safe paintbrush

Small bowl of water

Paper towels

White sanding sugar

1.  Fill a tipless piping bag with light green medium-consistency royal icing (see page 50) and use it to outline the cookie.

2.  Fill in the outline with the flood-consistency royal icing. Place the cookie in front of a tabletop fan for 30 minutes to begin the drying process. Then turn off the fan and allow it to dry completely, at least 8 to 12 hours.

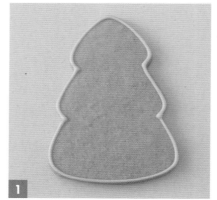

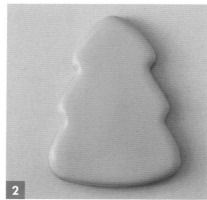

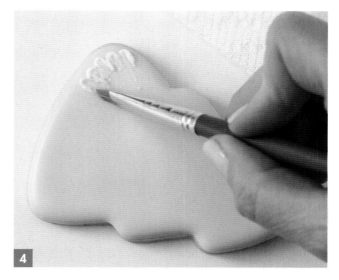

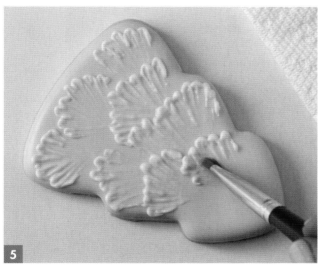

**3.** Fill a tipless piping bag with white stiff-consistency royal icing. You'll use the brushed embroidery technique to create the look of snowy branches on the tree (see page 70); remember to work quickly while the icing is still wet. Starting at the bottom of the tree, pipe the icing using a zigzag motion, covering a small section.

**4.** Dip the paintbrush in the bowl of water and blot it on a paper towel to remove excess moisture. Too much water on the brush will make the icing runny. Brush the icing downward using the edge of the brush, not the flat bristles.

**5.** Repeat steps 3 and 4, continuing to create small zigzag sections of icing until the tree is complete.

**6.** Sprinkle white sanding sugar over the freshly piped icing to create the look of glistening snow. The cookie should be ready for packaging within a few hours.

# SPRING COOKIES

## BUNNY WITH FLORAL CROWN

This adorable spring bunny cookie allows you to practice making a pretty royal icing springtime palette, creating the flowers, and arranging them to enhance the overall design.

### MATERIALS

Baked and cooled bunny face-shaped cookies

Edible ink pens, light brown and black, fine tip

Scribe tool

Tipless piping bags

Medium-consistency royal icing, pale pink and white (see page 47)

Flood-consistency royal icing, white (see page 47)

Assorted royal icing flowers in pale pastel colors (see pages 73 to 81)

Leaf piping tip

Stiff-consistency royal icing, pale green (see page 46)

Pink luster dust

Food-safe paintbrush

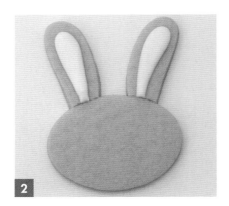

1. Mark a border between the ears and the face with a light brown edible ink pen. You can also use a scribe tool to etch a line between the sections.

2. Fill a tipless piping bag with medium-consistency pale pink icing (see page 50). Use the icing to outline and fill the center of the ears. Allow this section to crust over for a few minutes in front of a table fan. This will help prevent the icing from forming craters, or small indentations.

3. Fill tipless piping bags with medium- and flood-consistency white icing. Outline the remaining section of the ears with white medium-consistency icing and fill with the flood-consistency icing. Allow the icing to crust over.

4. Outline the face with white medium-consistency icing and fill with the flood-consistency icing. Allow the base to dry thoroughly for at least 8 to 12 hours, or overnight. The edible ink pen may puncture a hole in the icing if it's not completely dry.

5. Outline the inner ear around the pink section with medium-consistency white icing. This should set quickly.

I like arranging premade flowers on a cookie prior to gluing them in place. This ensures an appealing composition.

6. Create an assortment of royal icing flowers (see pages 73 to 81). They should include a variety of shapes, sizes, and colors, and be scaled to fit the cookie. I chose a pastel palette to represent spring. Pipe some medium-consistency white icing on the backs of the flowers and adhere them to the cookie.

*(continued)*

7. Once the flowers are secured in place, allow them to set for 20 to 30 minutes.

8. Fit a piping bag with the leaf piping tip and fill with stiff-consistency pale green icing. Pipe leaves next to the flowers (see page 76). Vary the position of the leaves and cluster some together in various spots.

9. Use a fine-tip black edible ink pen to draw the eyes and the mouth. A fine-tip pen creates a dainty look for this design. Draw two small dots for the eyes and a U shape with a line underneath for the mouth.

10. Create pink highlights on the bunny's cheeks by lightly swirling pink luster dust with a brush. Allow the cookie to dry for a few hours before handling it.

I like using a scribe tool to etch marks for the eye placement. This allows me to center and align the eyes before drawing them in pen. It would be a shame to get this far in the design process and mess up the cookie with wonky-placed eyes—I've done that many times, so I know!

# CARROT

This charming cookie is simple to decorate and makes a great addition to a collection of spring-themed cookies. Who knew that vegetables could be so tasty and look so pretty?

## MATERIALS

Baked and cooled carrot-shaped cookies

Tipless piping bags

Medium-consistency royal icing, orange (see page 47)

Flood-consistency royal icing, orange (see page 47)

Medium-consistency royal icing, green (see page 47)

Scribe tool

1. Fill tipless piping bags with medium-consistency orange icing and flood-consistency orange icing (see page 50). Outline the carrot with medium-consistency icing.

*(continued)*

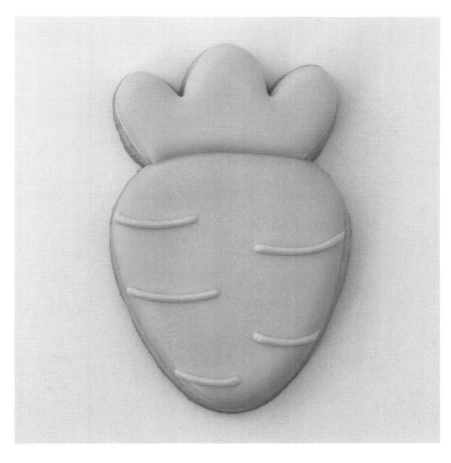

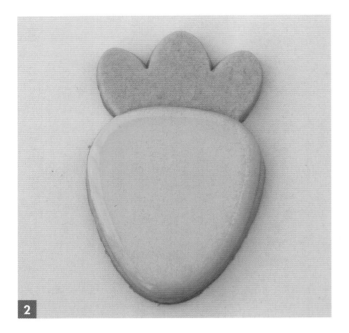

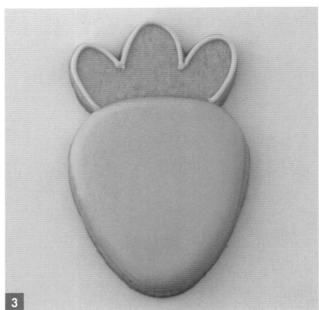

2. Fill the cookie with the flood-consistency icing. Place the cookie in front of a table fan until it's just crusted over, about 30 minutes.

3. Fill a tipless piping bag with medium-consistency green icing. Outline the leafy stem with the icing.

4. Fill in the leafy stem using the medium-consistency green icing. Pipe a few curved line details onto the carrot, using medium-consistency orange icing. Place the cookie in front of a table fan to allow the icing to set for a few hours and allow the cookie to fully dry for 8 to 12 hours, or overnight, prior to packaging.

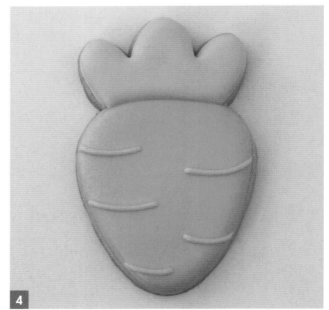

# BIRD

Dimensional layers of icing make this cherubic bird extra appealing, as does the springtime color palette.

**Note:** Very little orange and black icings are needed for this design, so make a small amount.

## MATERIALS

Baked and cooled bird-shaped cookies

Tipless piping bags

Medium- and flood-consistency royal icing, light blue (see page 47)

Edible ink pen, light brown

Scribe tool

Medium-consistency royal icing, black, orange, and pale green

1. Fill tipless piping bags with medium-consistency light blue icing and flood-consistency light blue icing (see page 50). Outline the bird with the medium-consistency icing, except for the beak.

*(continued)*

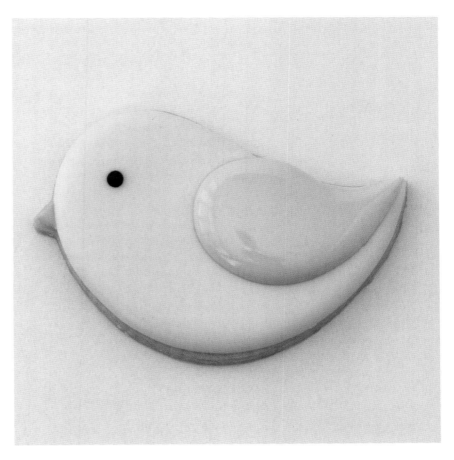

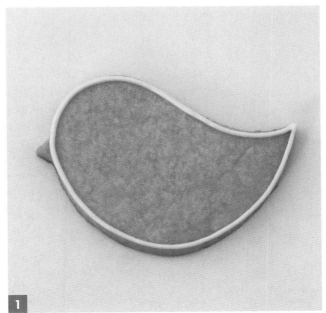

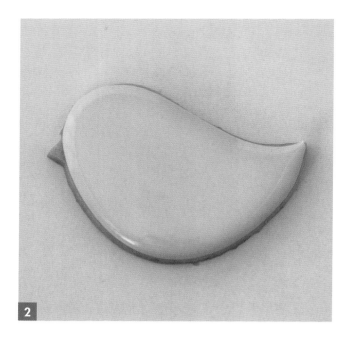

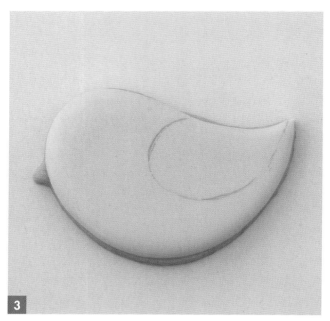

2. Fill in the body of the bird with the flood-consistency icing. Place the cookie in front of a table fan and allow the icing to fully dry, at least 8 to 12 hours, before moving on to the next step.

3. With the edible ink pen, draw a wing design on the bird that starts in the middle of the body and extends to the tail. You can use a scribe tool to mark the outline first, if you prefer.

4. Fill tipless piping bags with the medium-consistency black, orange, and green icings. Pipe on a small dot for the eye with the black icing. Pipe a triangular beak in orange. Pipe the outline of the wing with green icing, following the inked line. Hold the bag slightly over the cookie so the icing flows out and allows for a smooth, rounded shape.

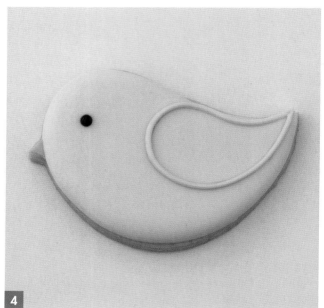

5. Apply a generous amount of green icing to the wing, adding more icing to the center (see finished cookie, page 103). This creates a puffy, dimensional look and will help prevent the icing from sinking in the middle as it dries. Immediately place the cookie in front of a table fan and allow it to dry for at least 8 to 12 hours prior to packaging.

# FLOWER WITH LEAVES

This flower is a simple design, but piping on swirly petal details lifts these cookies to a new level.

## MATERIALS

Baked and cooled flower and leaf-shaped cookies

Edible ink pen, light brown

Tipless piping bags

Medium-consistency royal icing, pink and green (see page 47)

Scribe tool

1. Draw the outline of the area between the flower and the leaves with the edible ink pen.

*(continued)*

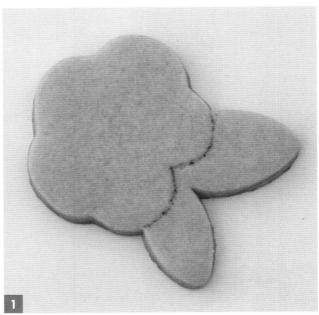

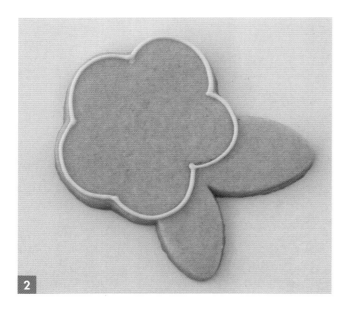

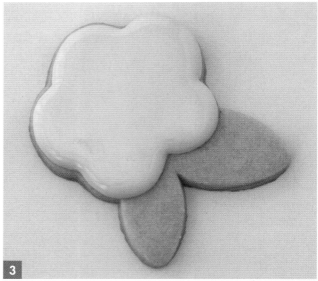

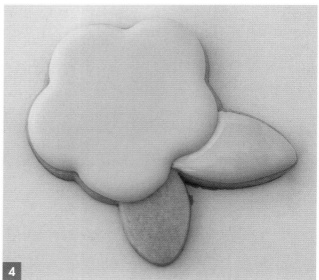

2. Fill tipless piping bags with the medium-consistency pink icing (see page 50). Outline the flower, going over the top of the inked line, with the medium-consistency icing.

3. Fill the flower, using the medium-consistency pink icing. If the cookie is larger than 2" (5 cm) in diameter, thin the icing to a flood consistency to make it easier to fill. Place the cookie in front of a table fan for about 20 minutes or until it crusts over.

4. Fill a tipless bag with the medium-consistency green icing and use it to outline and fill one of the leaves. Place the cookie in front of a table fan to crust over for 20 minutes. Be careful while handling the cookie, as the icing won't be fully dry and can be damaged. If you're not comfortable handling the cookie at this stage, you can let it dry for several hours between each step.

5. Outline and fill the second leaf the same way you did the first one. Add a wavy spiral to the flower using the medium-consistency pink icing. Hold the piping bag slightly above the surface, gently squeeze the bag, and pipe in a circular motion. By hovering just over the surface you'll get a smooth, flowing design (see finished cookie, page 105). Allow the cookie to dry for 8 to 12 hours, or overnight, prior to packaging.

# FLOWER BASKET

This cookie features the basketweave icing technique (see page 63) and royal icing flowers (see pages 73 to 81) to create a sweet container for a bouquet of spring blooms.

## MATERIALS

Baked and cooled basket-shaped cookies

Edible ink pen, light brown

Tipless piping bags

Basketweave piping tip #47

Stiff-consistency royal icing, white and light green (see page 46)

2-in-1 tool

Medium-consistency royal icing, white (see page 47)

Royal icing flowers in assorted sizes, shapes, and colors; the flowers should be thoroughly dry (see pages 73 to 81)

Leaf piping tip

1. Use a light brown edible ink pen to mark off the basket rim and handle.

2. Fit a piping bag with the basketweave #47 piping tip and fill with stiff-consistency white icing. Starting a little in from the left side, place the piping tip flat against the cookie surface and pipe a vertical line from the bottom of the basket rim to the bottom of the basket, using steady pressure.

*(continued)*

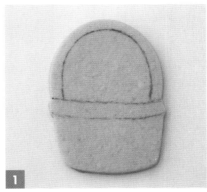

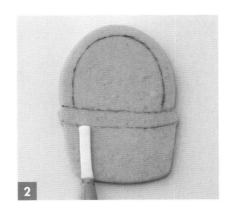

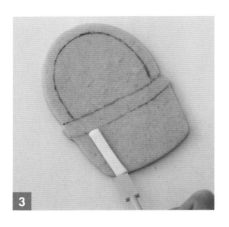 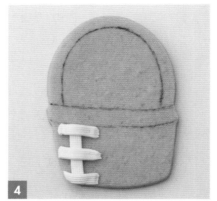 

3. Use a 2-in-1 tool to smooth the icing at the base of the basket.

4. Pipe evenly spaced horizontal lines over the vertical lines (see page 64). Make sure that the spaces between the lines are slightly larger than the piping tip. Clean up any edges with the 2-in-1 tool.

5. Pipe another vertical line just over the edges of the horizontal lines, again leaving a space between the lines that's slightly larger than the piping tip.

6. Pipe another row of horizontal lines between the vertical ones.

7. Repeat steps 2 through 6 until the entire basket is covered below the rim.

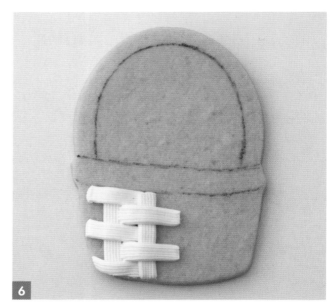

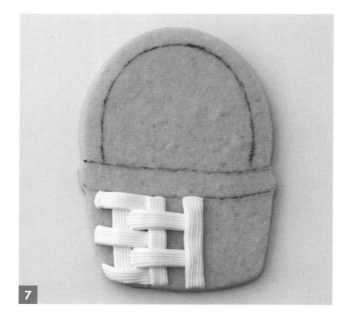

Maintain steady pressure while piping with stiff icing, or the icing may stop mid-flow.

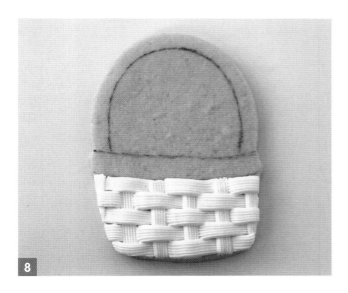

**8.** This is how the completed basketweave section should look. The stiff-consistency icing sets quickly, so you can move on to the next step immediately.

**9.** Fill a tipless piping bag with medium-consistency white icing. Outline and flood the basket rim. Place the cookie in front of a table fan and allow it to crust over for at least 20 minutes. Pipe horizontal lines on the basket rim using the medium-consistency white icing. Outline and flood the handle with medium-consistency white icing. Allow the cookie to set in front of a table fan for at least 6 hours before applying the royal icing flowers to the basket.

**10.** Pipe a small dot of icing on the back of the flowers and gently press them onto the cookie. Leave a small space between the flowers for piping leaves.

**11.** Fit a piping bag with a leaf tip and fill with stiff-consistency green icing. Begin piping the leaves at the edges of the flowers and go outward (see page 77). Pipe the leaves at different angles, individually and in clusters. Allow the cookie to thoroughly dry for 8 to 12 hours, or overnight, before packaging.

# SUMMER COOKIES

# SURFBOARD

The colors of summer shine in this vibrant surfboard cookie. Use the wet-on-wet technique (see page 58) to create a funky floral design that coordinates perfectly with the Hawaiian shirt (see page 112).

**Note:** Very little orange, lime green, and pink icings are needed for this design, so make small amounts of each.

### MATERIALS

Baked and cooled surfboard-shaped cookies

Edible ink pen, light brown

Tipless piping bags

Medium-consistency royal icing, turquoise and yellow (see page 47)

Flood-consistency royal icing, white, orange, lime green, and pink (see page 47)

Scribe tool

1. Mark off a design on the surfboard cookie using the light brown edible ink pen. I created a simple wavy color block pattern, making sure to leave ample space in the middle for the wet-on-wet floral design.

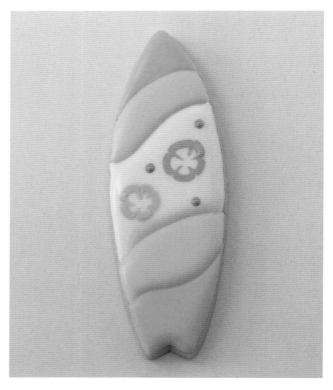

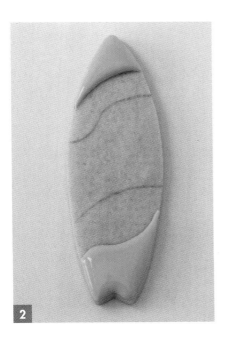

**2**   **3**   **4**

2. Fill tipless piping bags with all of the medium- and flood-consistency royal icings (see page 50). Use the medium-consistency turquoise icing to outline and fill the two sections at either end of the surfboard. Allow the icing to crust over for about 20 minutes.

3. Outline and fill the adjoining sections with medium-consistency yellow icing and allow it to crust over for about 20 minutes.

4. The middle section will be a wet-on-wet technique (see page 58). Make sure the icing bags are ready to go and move quickly. Outline the white with medium-consistency icing, then flood the center. Immediately pipe orange and lime green circles.

5. Immediately use the scribe tool to drag the icing inward to create flowers.

6. Pipe on pink dots while the white base is still wet (see the finished cookie, opposite). Let the cookie dry for 8 to 12 hours, or overnight, before packaging.

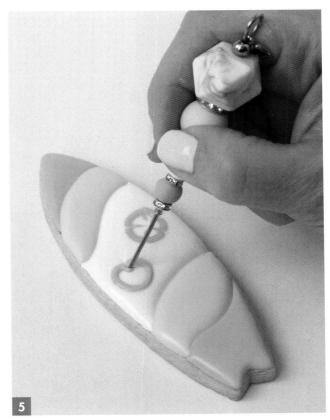

**5**

# HAWAIIAN SHIRT

These cookies pack a big wow factor, but they incorporate easy techniques for making wet-on-wet flowers (see page 58). Using complementary colors of turquoise and orange boosts the summer vibe.

**Note:** Very little orange and white icings are needed for this design, so make small amounts of each.

## MATERIALS

Baked and cooled shirt-shaped cookies

Tipless piping bags

Medium-consistency royal icing, turquoise (see page 47)

Flood-consistency royal icing, turquoise, white, and orange (see page 47)

Scribe tool

1. The shirt will be a wet-on-wet technique as shown on page 58. So, we have to have our icing bags ready to go and move quickly. Fill tipless piping bags with all of the medium- and flood-consistency royal icings (see page 50). Use the medium-consistency turquoise icing to outline the shirt.

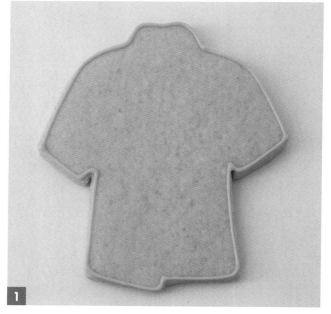

SUMMER COOKIES

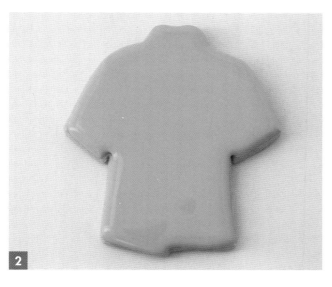

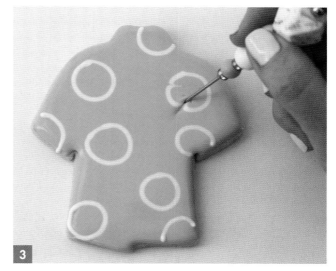

**2.** Immediately use the flood-consistency turquoise icing to fill the outline.

**3.** Immediately pipe circles on the shirt with flood-consistency white icing. Use the scribe tool to drag the icing inward to create a flower. This step needs to be done quickly as the icing begins to set within a minute.

**4.** Pipe on orange dots throughout to fill in negative space. Allow the base to dry for at least 6 to 8 hours prior to moving on to the next step.

**5.** Using medium-consistency turquoise icing, pipe an outline of a pocket and collar.

**6.** Flood the pocket area and collar using medium-consistency turquoise icing to add dimension (see the finished cookie, opposite). Place in front of a table fan immediately. This will help prevent craters and dips in the small sections. Allow the cookie to fully dry for at least 6 to 8 hours, or overnight, prior to packaging.

# FLIP-FLOPS

No summer outing is complete without a pair of flip-flops. These feature polka dots made with the wet-on-wet technique (see page 58) and a pink fondant flower (see page 82). They're chic enough to wear *and* eat!

## MATERIALS

Baked and cooled flip-flop-shaped cookies

Tipless piping bags

Medium- and flood-consistency royal icing, orange (see page 47)

Flood-consistency royal icing, white (see page 47)

Medium-consistency royal icing, lime green (see page 47)

Scribe tool

Pink fondant flower (see page 78)

1. The flip-flop will be a wet-on-wet technique as shown on page 58. So, we have to have our flood-consistency icing bags ready to go and move quickly. Fill tipless piping bags with medium- and flood-consistency orange and white flood-consistency royal icings (see page 50). Use the medium-consistency orange icing to outline the flip-flop.

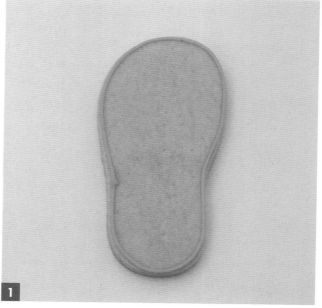

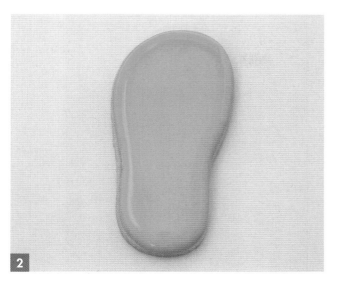

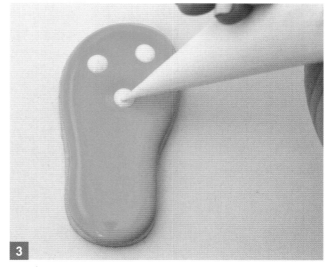

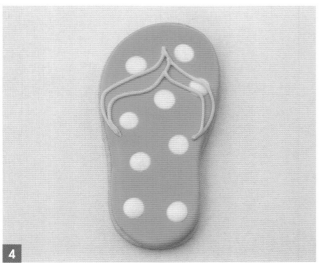

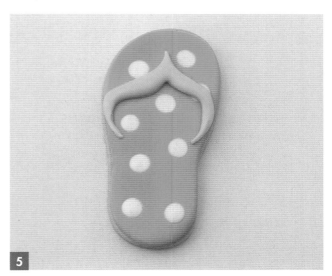

2. Immediately flood the cookie using flood-consistency orange icing.

3. Immediately pipe random polka dots with flood-consistency white icing. Allow the cookie to dry for at least 6 to 8 hours prior to moving on to the next step. You will still have to be careful handling the cookie at that point as it will not be fully dry.

4. Fill a tipless piping bag with the medium-consistency green icing and use it to outline the straps. Let it set for 1 minute.

5. Fill in the straps using the same medium-consistency green icing. Use the scribe tool to smooth out the icing if necessary. Using a medium-consistency icing is best as these small areas are prone to craters. If you find the medium too thick for your comfort, thin it out slightly. Allow the straps to dry for at least 6 hours.

6. To finish off this design, gently adhere the fondant flower to the straps with medium-consistency green icing, as the cookie is not fully dry (see finished cookie, opposite). Allow the cookie to dry thoroughly for at least 8 to 12 hours, or overnight, prior to packaging.

# BATHING SUIT

It's official: Bathing suit season must include cookies. These pretty, color-blocked treats are perfect for your next pool party.

## MATERIALS

Baked and cooled bathing suit–shaped cookies

Edible ink pen, light brown

Tipless piping bags

Medium-consistency royal icing, pink, green, and white (see page 47)

Scribe tool

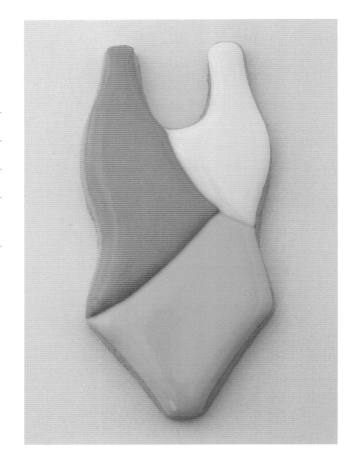

1. Draw out the sections using an edible food pen. Fill tipless piping bags with all the medium-consistency icings (see page 50), as these are small sections. If the icing is too thick to work with, fill using flood-consistency icing. Outline the first section with pink icing.

2. Flood the outline using the same pink icing. Let this section crust over for about 15 minutes.

3. Outline and flood the next section in green and allow it to crust over for another 15 minutes.

4. Outline and flood the last section in white (see the finished cookie, this page). Let the cookie dry for at least 8 to 12 hours, or overnight, prior to packaging.

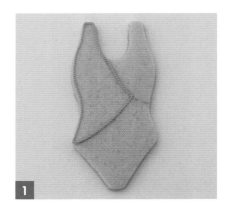
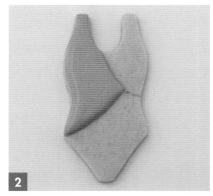
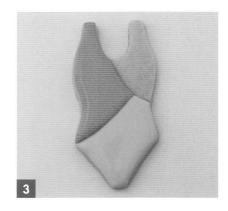

# BEACH AND SHELLS

This dynamic cookie is filled with texture, color, and dimension and will remind you of fun times strolling on the beach. Create sand with cookie shavings and make foamy waves using the brushed embroidery technique (see page 70).

## MATERIALS

Baked and cooled rectangle-shaped cookies

Tipless piping bags

Medium- and flood-consistency light brown and turquoise icing (see page 47)

Stiff-consistency royal icing, white (see page 46)

Cookie shavings (see page 16)

Small food-grade paintbrush

Square-tip food-grade paintbrush

Small bowl of water

Paper towels

Molded white fondant seashells (see page 82)

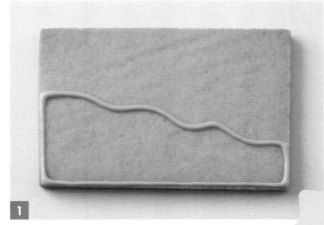

1. Fill tipless piping bags with medium- and flood-consistency light brown and turquoise icing (see page 50). With light brown medium-consistency icing, outline the sand section of the cookie. Pipe using an up-and-down flowing motion to create gentle waves.

Add a tiny amount of green food coloring to the brown icing to eliminate a red hue.

*(continued)*

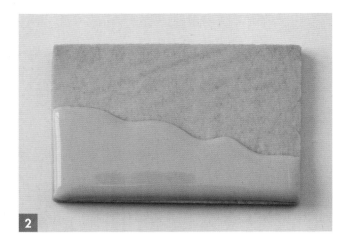

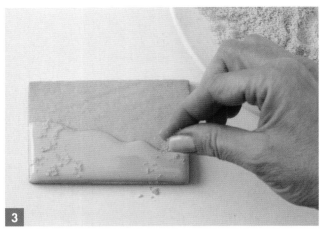

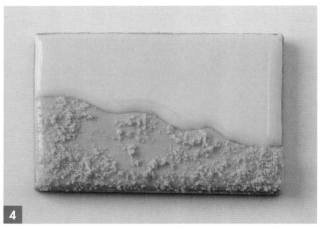

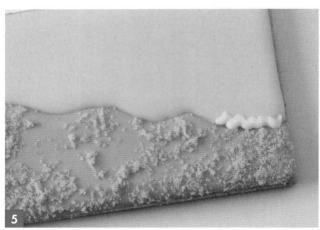

**2.** Immediately flood the sand area using flood-consistency light brown icing.

**3.** While the icing is still wet, sprinkle some cookie shavings in random spots to create a sandy effect. Use a small paintbrush to dust any shavings off the bare cookie.

**4.** Outline the water section of the cookie using medium-consistency turquoise icing, then fill using the flood-consistency turquoise icing. Allow the cookie to dry for at least 8 to 12 hours, up to overnight, prior to moving on to the next step.

**5.** Fill a tipless piping bag with stiff-consistency white royal icing. Pipe a small section of icing in a zigzag motion, in between the sand and water.

**6.** Dip the square-tip brush in the bowl of water, then blot excess moisture off both sides of the brush on a paper towel. With the brush held flat against the cookie, brush the white icing in a downwards motion over the turquoise icing (see page 71). Working quickly is necessary so the icing doesn't dry.

**7.** Adjust the position of the paintbrush to create a slightly different look in the water—a foam-like appearance. Randomly pipe small white zigzags throughout the water area. Dip the brush in water and blot on the paper towel. Then, holding the brush at a 90-degree angle, dot the brush into the icing and repeat until you achieve the desired effect.

**8.** Repeat steps 6 and 7 throughout the water section of the cookie, adding more waves and foam toward the sand.

**9.** Pipe a small amount of white icing on the back of the molded fondant shells. Apply the shells to the sand area and press down with gentle pressure. Allow the shells to dry in place for at least 3 hours prior to packaging.

# STARFISH

Another way to incorporate dots on cookies is to make them 3-D. This bright pink starfish gets its bumpy look from piped icing that creates a dimensional surface.

## MATERIALS

Baked and cooled starfish-shaped cookies

Tipless piping bags

Medium-consistency royal icing, hot pink (see page 47)

Flood-consistency royal icing, hot pink (see page 47)

1. Fill tipless piping bags with the pink icings (see page 50). Outline the cookie with the medium-consistency pink icing.

2. Flood the outline using the flood-consistency pink icing. Allow the base to dry for at least 6 hours prior to piping on the details. The cookie will be crusted over enough after 6 hours for small details, but not fully dry, so be mindful when handling.

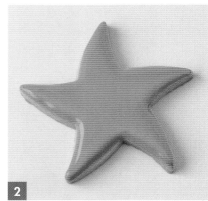

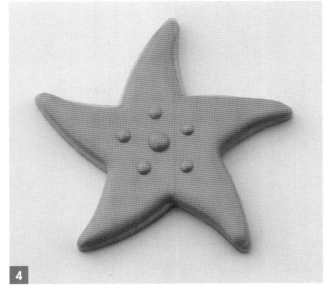

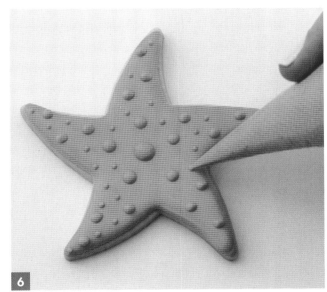

3.  Using medium-consistency pink icing, pipe a large dot in the center of the cookie.

4.  Pipe five smaller dots around the center dot.

5.  Continue to pipe more dots down the sides. Try to keep them consistent in size.

6.  Using the same piping bag, release pressure while squeezing and pipe small dots throughout the open spaces. Depending on how thin your icing is, you may not even have to apply any pressure to your piping bag. Sometimes you can just allow it to flow out without squeezing and dot it onto the cookie.

7.  Once you finish piping all of the dots, allow the cookie to dry completely for 8 to 12 hours, or overnight, prior to packaging.

# FALL COOKIES

## LEAFY BRANCH

If there's one motif that epitomizes fall, it's leaves. These cookies were decorated with green leaves, but you can easily incorporate other seasonal colors, such as orange, red, and yellow.

### MATERIALS

Baked and cooled leafy branch-shaped cookies

Tipless piping bags

Medium- and flood-consistency royal icing, white (see page 47)

Medium-consistency royal icing, brown and green (see page 47)

1. Fill a tipless piping bag with the medium-consistency white icing (see page 50). Outline the cookie with the icing.

2. Flood the outline using the flood-consistency white icing. Place the cookie in front of a table fan to begin the drying process. Allow the base to dry for at least 6 to 8 hours prior to moving on to the next step. Be careful while handling the cookie as it will not be fully dry, but it will be set enough to pipe the branch and leaves.

3. Fill tipless piping bags with the medium-consistency brown and green icings. With the brown icing, outline the branch and immediately fill the outline. Place in front of a table fan to crust over for about 20 minutes.

4. Using the green icing, outline the leaves.

5. Flood the leaves using the same green icing. Be generous with the icing; fill the center of each leaf with extra icing. This will help prevent dipping and create a puffy appearance (see finished cookie, opposite). After filling all of the leaves, allow the cookie to fully dry for at least 8 to 12 hours, or overnight, prior to packaging.

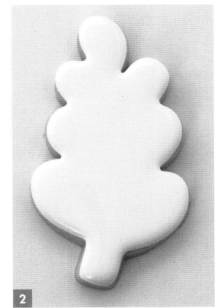

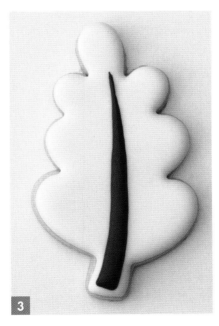

# RUSTIC WREATH

This seasonal wreath gets a pop of color from four rosette icing flowers that can be made ahead. Include this cookie in your repertoire during other seasons, too, merely by switching out the flowers and color palette. If you can't find a wreath cookie cutter, cut a scalloped circle and use a smaller round cookie cutter to cut a hole in the center.

## MATERIALS

Baked and cooled scalloped-edge wreath-shaped cookies

Tipless piping bags

Medium-consistency royal icing, white (see page 47)

Flood-consistency royal icing, white (see page 47)

Piping-consistency royal icing, brown (see page 46)

Scribe tool

3 to 5 mini rosettes, any color (see page 74)

Leaf tip #67

Stiff-consistency royal icing, green (see page 46)

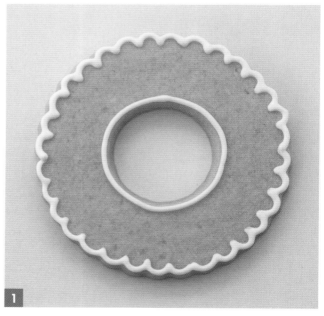

When piping scalloped edges, use a piping- or medium-consistency royal icing. This will prevent the icing from spilling off the edges and help maintain the scallop shape.

1. Fill a tipless piping bag with the medium-consistency white icing (see page 50). Outline the scalloped edges and center cutout with the icing.

FALL COOKIES

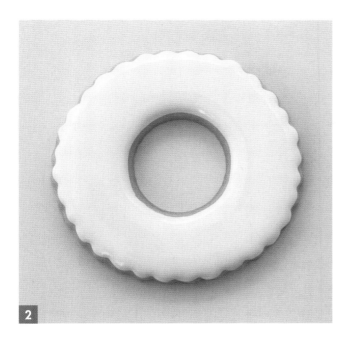

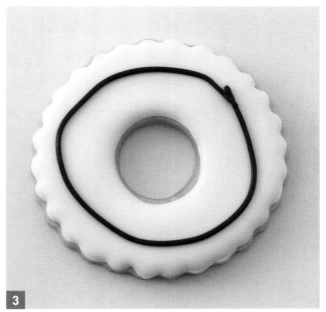

2. Fill a tipless piping bag with the flood-consistency white icing. Fill in the outlined cookie with the icing. Place in front of a table fan for at least ½ hour to begin the drying process, then allow the cookie to fully dry for 8 to 12 hours, or overnight, prior to moving on to the next step.

3. Fill a tipless piping bag with the piping-consistency brown icing. Pipe an asymmetrical circle in the middle of the wreath. It does not have to be perfectly round. (You can use a scribe tool to mark the outline first if you prefer.)

4. Pipe two or three more asymmetrical circles, overlapping each other. Pipe on more circles if you have a larger cookie that allows for more space.

*(continued)*

5

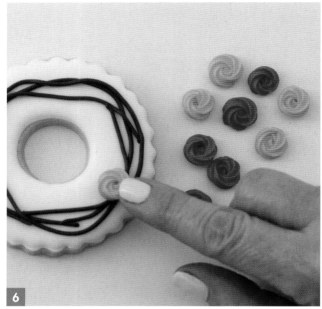

6

7

8

**5.** Pipe a small amount of brown icing on to the back of each flower to act as the "glue."

**6.** Gently press the flowers onto the wreath.

**7.** Add as many flowers as you like. If your cookie is large, add more to fill the space.

**8.** Fit a piping bag with the leaf tip (see page 76) and fill with the stiff-consistency green icing. Pipe leaves in between the flowers at different angles to add dimension (see page 77). Allow the flowers and leaves to set in place for at least 6 hours prior to packaging.

# SUNFLOWER

These bold blooms feature a subtle ombre effect on the petals, courtesy of some petal dust. The sanding sugar in the middle of the flower adds great texture and a nice crunch.

## MATERIALS

Baked and cooled sunflower-shaped cookies

Tipless piping bags

Medium-consistency royal icing, yellow and dark brown (see page 47)

Flood-consistency royal icing, yellow (see page 47)

Round cookie cutter or any other circular shape to trace the center of the sunflower

Edible food pen, brown

Orange petal dust

Food-grade paintbrush

Bowl filled with brown sanding sugar

1. Fill a tipless piping bag with the medium-consistency yellow icing (see page 47). Outline the sunflower with the icing.

*(continued)*

2. Fill a tipless piping bag with the flood-consistency yellow icing. Fill the entire cookie with the icing. Place in front of a table fan for at least ½ hour to begin the drying process, then allow the cookie to dry for 8 to 12 hours, or overnight; the cookie base should be completely dry before moving on to the next step.

3. Outline the center of the sunflower using a round cookie cutter and the edible food pen.

4. Apply the orange petal dust using a paintbrush around the center outline. Brush the dust slightly toward the petals.

5

6

5. Fill a tipless piping bag with the medium-consistency brown icing and pipe over the food pen outline.

6. Immediately fill the center using the same medium-consistency brown icing.

7. With the center freshly flooded, turn the cookie upside down and gently dip the center into the sanding sugar. Allow the center to dry for 6 to 12 hours, or until completely dry, prior to packaging.

7

# SUGAR SKULL

These bold, colorful sugar skull cookies are popular around Halloween and so fun to make. Create eye-catching works of art with vibrant colors and textures, courtesy of fondant flowers and edible glitter.

## MATERIALS

Baked and cooled skull-shaped cookies

Edible food pen, black

Scribe tool

Food-grade straight-edge paintbrush

Medium-consistency royal icing, black (see page 47)

Edible glitter, black or color of your choice

Tipless piping bags

Medium-consistency royal icing, white (see page 47)

Flood-consistency royal icing, white (see page 47)

Fondant flowers and leaves in assorted colors (see page 82)

Pink petal dust

THE BEGINNER'S GUIDE TO COOKIE DECORATING

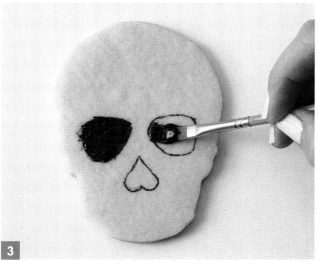

1. With the edible food pen, trace outlines on the cookie where you want the eyes. You can also use a scribe tool to etch the shapes. Don't worry if they're not perfect, as you will be covering them up in step 3.

2. Next, outline the shape of the nose. You can flip the cookie upside down and draw a heart.

3. Dip the paintbrush in medium-consistency black icing and apply the icing inside the eyes and nose. It's okay to go outside of the lines, as it will be covered up.

4. Spray edible glitter onto the eyes and nose right after it is painted so it can adhere to the royal icing. This will create a vibrant and shimmery effect. If you are decorating multiple cookies, you can use different colors of glitter. I used black, red, and blue glitter on my cookies.

*(continued)*

5. Fill tipless piping bags with the medium- and flood-consistency white icings (see page 50). Outline the eyes and nose with the medium-consistency icing. Let it crust over for 1 minute.

6. Outline the face with medium-consistency white icing, then fill with flood-consistency white icing. The base is complete and needs to be completely dry prior to adding details with your edible food pen. Allow the cookie to dry for 8 to 12 hours, or overnight, prior to moving on to the next step.

7. Create a floral crown using fondant flowers and leaves. Use medium-consistency white icing to adhere the fondant flowers and leaves to the cookie.

Arrange the flowers and leaves on the cookie prior to gluing them on to ensure they fit nicely and are aesthetically pleasing.

8. Use an assortment of shapes and sizes and layer the flowers on top of the leaves.

9. You're going to make happy sugar skulls, so use the edible food pen to draw a smile. You can always make a scarier version just by changing the shape of the mouth and eyes.

10. Gently swirl your paintbrush with pink petal dust to create rosy cheeks.

11. Allow the fondant flowers to set on the cookie for 1 hour or until they no longer slide around the cookie surface.

# GHOST

These ghosts are perfect for Halloween and can be friendly or scary depending on how you decorate the face.

**Note:** Very little black icing is needed for this design, so make a small amount.

## MATERIALS

Baked and cooled ghost-shaped cookies

Tipless piping bags

Medium-consistency royal icing, white and black (see page 47)

Flood-consistency royal icing, white (see page 47)

Scribe tool

1. Fill tipless piping bags with the medium- and flood-consistency white icings (see page 50). Outline the cookie with the medium-consistency icing and flood the cookie with the flood-consistency white icing.

2. Place the cookie in front of a table fan to begin the drying process and let dry for at least 3 hours. The icing does not need to be completely dry to add the details because they are small and not heavy. Be careful while handling the cookie when you move on to steps 2 and 3, as it will not be fully dry and you can easily damage the icing.

3. Use medium-consistency white icing to outline the entire cookie.

4. Fill a tipless piping bag with the medium-consistency black icing. Pipe on two small black dots for the eyes, then immediately pipe smaller white reflections into the eyes using the medium-consistency white icing and the wet-on-wet technique (see page 58). (You can use a scribe tool to mark the placement of the eyes first, if desired.) Add additional movement to the ghost by piping waves into the arms and base with medium-consistency white icing (see finished cookie, opposite page). Let the cookie dry for 8 to 12 hours, or overnight, prior to packaging.

# 4

# CELEBRATION COOKIES

The decorated cookies in this chapter are so versatile that they can be made for any special occasion. The cake can take center stage at a wedding or a birthday, while the flower bouquet is perfect for Mother's Day or a welcome home party. Make the hamburger and hot dog look-alike cookies for Father's Day or your next family reunion barbecue. If there's a party, celebrate with cookies!

# MOTHER'S DAY BOUQUET

Although mothers should be celebrated every day for their unconditional love and sacrifices, we pay special honor to them one day a year. Instead of giving flowers, decorate this stunning cookie bouquet. She'll admire its beauty and indulge in a sweet treat. This bouquet is versatile enough to make for a birthday or wedding shower. I recommend using medium-consistency royal icing when decorating florals; the sections are generally small enough to allow for quick flooding. It also creates a nice puffy petal!

## MATERIALS

Edible food pen, light brown

Tipless piping bags

Scribe tool

**For the vase:**

Baked and cooled vase-shaped cookies

Medium-consistency royal icing, pale blue (see page 47)

Flood-consistency royal icing, pale blue (see page 47)

**For the leaf:**

Baked and cooled leaf-shaped cookies

Medium-consistency royal icing, pale green (see page 47)

Leafy Branch leaves (see pages 122 to 123)

**For the flowers:**

Baked and cooled assorted flower-shaped cookies

Medium-consistency royal icing, bright pink, light pink, coral, and white (see page 47)

Food-grade paintbrush

Petal dust, dark pink, medium pink, and dark coral (optional)

Round royal icing transfers, yellow (see page 61)

Edible food pen, black, fine tip

Piping-consistency royal icing, coral (see page 46)

Cornstarch (optional)

## Vase

1. Fill a tipless piping bag with medium-consistency pale blue icing (see page 50). Outline the base of the vase using medium-consistency pale blue royal icing then flood using flood-consistency royal icing. Place in front of a cool fan until it crusts over (approximately 15 minutes).

2. Use the same medium-consistency icing to outline then flood to fill the top section of the vase. Allow the cookie to fully dry overnight. Once completely dry, use petal dust and a brush to dust in the crease to create dimension.

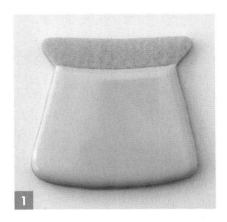

## Leaf

1. Use an edible food pen to trace the sections on the leaf. I drew a wavy line down the center.

2. Fill a tipless piping bag with medium-consistency pale green icing (see page 50). Outline and flood one side of the leaf. Place the cookie in front of a table fan to crust over for 15 to 20 minutes. Be mindful when moving on to the next step that the cookie is still wet; grip from the base of the cookie to move it.

3. Outline and flood the other side of the leaf. Place it in front of a table fan to begin the drying process. Allow the cookie to fully dry for at least 8 to 12 hours, or overnight, prior to packaging.

## Bright Pink Flower

1. Use an edible food pen to mark a dot in the center of the cookie and then draw the petals from that center point.

2. Fill a tipless piping bag with medium-consistency bright pink icing (see page 50). Outline and flood the first petal. Pipe a generous amount of icing in the center of the petals; this will help prevent the royal icing from dipping and cratering. Place in front of a table fan immediately so it begins to crust over; 15 minutes should be sufficient.

3. Repeat step 2 for each additional petal. Place in front of a table fan to dry for at least 15 minutes, then allow the cookie to fully dry for 6 to 8 hours prior to moving to the next step. If using petal dust, allow the cookie to fully dry 8 to 12 hours or overnight.

4. With a paintbrush, dust the center of the cookie, including in between each petal, with petal dust that is slightly darker than your royal icing (this step is completely optional). Pipe straight lines, overlapping one another, in the center of the cookie using the medium-consistency bright pink icing.

5. Pipe a small amount of icing onto the back of the yellow circle transfer and press in place in the center of the flower. Allow the cookie to fully dry for 8 to 12 hours, or overnight, prior to packaging.

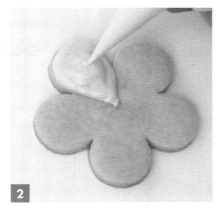

## Light Pink Flower

1.  Use an edible food pen to mark a dot in the center of the cookie and then draw the petals from that center point.

2.  Fill a tipless piping bag with medium-consistency light pink icing (see page 50). Outline and flood the first petal. Pipe a generous amount of icing in the center of the petals; this will help prevent the royal icing from dipping and cratering. Place in front of a table fan immediately so it begins to crust over; 15 minutes should be sufficient.

3.  Outline and flood alternating petals, allowing them to crust over before moving to the next one.

4.  Place in front of a table fan to dry for at least 15 minutes, then allow the cookie to fully dry for 6 to 8 hours prior to moving to the next step. If using petal dust, allow the cookie to fully dry 8 to 12 hours or overnight.

5.  For added dimension, brush on some petal dust in between each petal, concentrating more in the center of the flower. Use petal dust that is slightly darker than your royal icing (this step is completely optional). Pipe a small amount of icing onto the back of the yellow circle transfer and press in place in the center of the flower. Allow the cookie to fully dry for 8 to 12 hours, or overnight, prior to packaging.

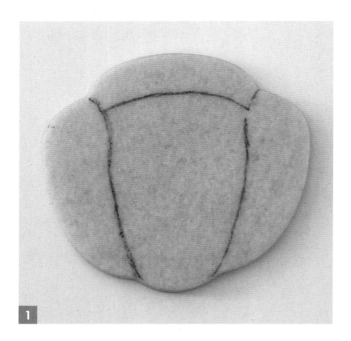

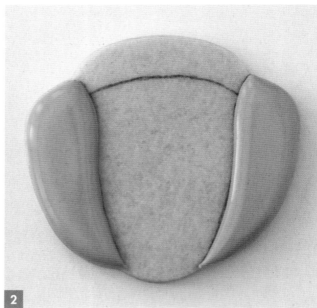

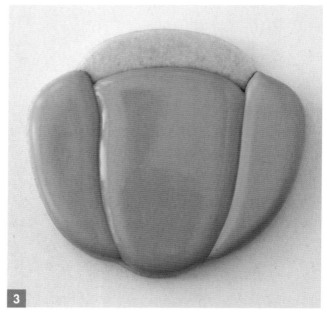

## Coral Flower

1.  Use an edible food pen to outline the three sections of petals.

2.  Fill tipless piping bags with medium-consistency coral and white icings (see page 50). Outline and flood the outer petals with coral icing. Place in front of a table fan and allow the icing to crust over for about 15 minutes prior to moving on to the next step.

3.  Outline and flood the center petal with coral icing. Again, place in front of a fan to crust over for 15 minutes.

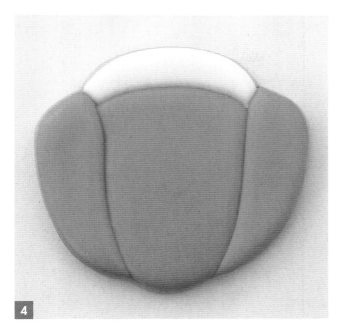

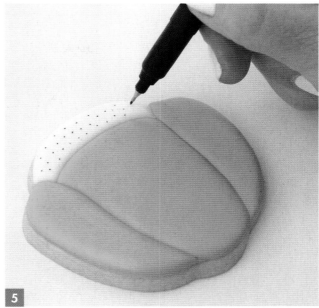

4. Outline and flood the top portion of the cookie with white icing. Allow the cookie to completely dry overnight prior to adding details. If the icing is not fully dry, the marker will puncture it in the next step.

5. Use a fine-tip black edible food pen to add dots to the top portion of the cookie.

6. Use a brush to add petal dust to the creases of the petals. Then use piping-consistency coral icing to pipe details on the base of the petals. You can use a scribe tool to mark the placement, if desired. Allow the details to dry for at least 2 hours. If the dots still appear wet after some time has passed, dust the area lightly with cornstarch prior to packaging.

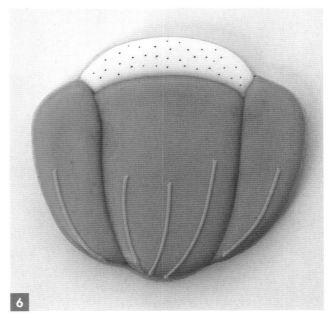

# FATHER'S DAY HAMBURGER

Celebrate Dad on Father's Day with these cookies that look just like a hamburger. Getting the kids or grandkids involved in creating them would make this perfect gift even better. These cookies are also ideal for your favorite fast-food foodie.

**Note:** To achieve the light brown color of the hamburger bun, I used a mixture of ivory and brown colorants. Getting the right color of the hot dog can be tricky. To achieve this color, I mixed red and avocado food colorants, then added a little bit of brown. To create a dark chocolate royal icing, mix a small amount of black colorant into your brown icing. Very little ivory icing is needed for this design, so make a small amount.

## MATERIALS

Edible food pens, brown and black

Tipless piping bags

Scribe tool

**For the hamburger:**

Baked and cooled burger-shaped cookies

Medium- and flood-consistency royal icing, light brown (see page 47) (see Note, opposite)

Stiff-consistency royal icing, dark brown (see page 46)

Medium-consistency royal icing, bright green, red, yellow, and ivory (see page 47)

**For the hot dog:**

Baked and cooled hot-dog–shaped cookies

Medium-consistency royal icing, ivory and meat color (see page 47) (see Note, opposite)

Medium-consistency royal icing, red (see page 47)

1. Use a brown edible food pen to outline the buns on the burger.

2. Fill tipless piping bags with the medium- and flood-consistency light brown icings (see page 50). Outline the top and bottom bun portions with medium-consistency light brown icing then fill with flood-consistency light brown icing. Place in front of a table fan and allow to dry for at least 8 to 12 hours, or overnight, prior to moving on to the next step. Fill tipless piping bags with the remainder of the icings after the cookies have dried (see page 50).

*(continued)*

If you're not using petal dust to add highlights to the bun, you can move to step 4 within 30 minutes. The cookie will need to crust over prior to icing the meat portion. When using petal dust, the surface needs to be completely dry and would therefore require additional drying time.

**3**    **4**

3. To create a more realistic bun, brush brown petal dust on the edges of the bun. In a back-and-forth motion, dust just the edges.

4. Pipe on the meat portion of the burger using the stiff-consistency dark brown icing. We want this section to be textured, so a stiffer consistency is best. This part of the decorating process is easy because you don't have to pipe it on neatly! Pipe in a wave-like pattern on the top section and in a wavy pattern on the bottom. Place in front of a fan and allow the icing to crust over for 20 minutes.

5. For the lettuce, pipe on medium-consistency green icing just above the meat. Just below the meat, pipe on medium-consistency red icing for the ketchup. Only pipe on the outer sections, as the middle will be the cheese. Place in front of a fan to crust over for 20 minutes.

**5**

6. Pipe on the small middle section using medium-consistency yellow icing for the cheese. Use your scribe tool to drag down the cheese in the bottom corners into a defined point and give the illusion of melting cheese.

7. To create sesame seeds on the top portion of the bun, pipe a few small dots of medium-consistency ivory icing.

8. Immediately after piping the dots, from the center of the dot, use a scribe tool to drag the icing outward to form a point. Drag your icing in random directions for every dot so it looks more realistic. Repeat to add more sesame seeds to the bun.

9. Your delicious-looking burger is complete (see finished cookie, page 144). Allow the details to completely dry for at least 6 hours prior to packaging.

10. Follow the same basic directions for the hamburger to create the hot dog. The buns are the same technique on both cookies. After the hot dog (meat portion) is outlined and filled, it has to dry for 8 to 12 hours or overnight if you'd like to draw on the grill lines with a black edible ink pen. You can add squiggly lines in yellow or red for condiments (mustard or ketchup).

# WEDDING/ANNIVERSARY CAKE

Every celebration needs a cake—or a cake on a cookie! The colors of this elegant cookie work well for a wedding or an anniversary, but change them up and add more flowers and you have the perfect indulgence for a birthday.

**Note:** Very little pale green icing is needed for this design, so make a small amount.

## MATERIALS

Baked and cooled plaque-shaped cookies

Tipless piping bags

Piping-consistency royal icing, pale blue, white, and pale green (see page 46)

Square-shaped royal icing transfer, white (see page 61)

Flood-consistency royal icing, pale blue (see page 47)

Scribe tool

Gold luster dust

Paint palette

High-content alcohol or clear vanilla extract (to paint the dust)

Food-grade paintbrush

Premade royal icing mini rosette, white (see page 74)

Small leaf piping tip

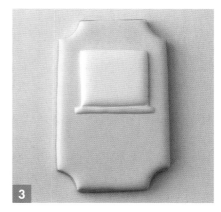

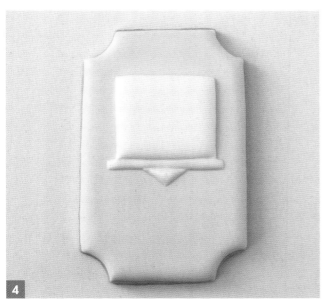

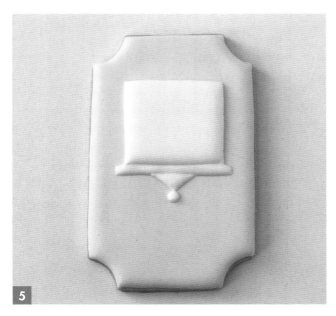

1. Fill a tipless piping bag with the piping- and flood-consistency light blue icings (see page 50). Use the piping-consistency icing to pipe the outline of the cookie, then flood the outline with the flood-consistency icing. Allow it to fully dry for 8 to 12 hours, or overnight. Once the base is fully dry, fill a tipless piping bag with the medium-consistency white icing, then pipe some icing onto the back of the square royal icing transfer.

2. Position the transfer on the upper section of the cookie, then gently push into place.

3. With the medium-consitency white icing, pipe a thin rectangular shape just below the square cake. (You can use a scribe tool to etch the outline for the cake stand, if desired.) This will be the cake stand. Place in front of a table fan and allow this section to just crust over, 5 to 10 minutes.

4. With the white icing, pipe a triangular shape in the middle of the cake base. Again, place in front of a table fan to crust over for a few minutes.

5. Just below the triangle, pipe a circle. Place in front of a table fan for a few minutes.

*(continued)*

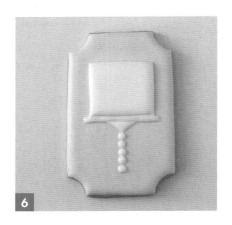
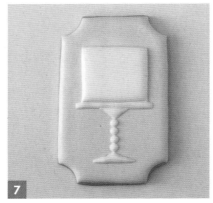
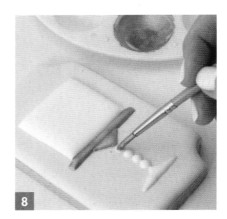

6. Repeat step 5 to pipe a total of five circles and let crust over for a few minutes.

7. Pipe another elongated triangle at the bottom of the cake stand. Allow the details to dry for at least 2 to 4 hours before painting the cake stand with the luster dust. The table fan will speed up the process.

8. Mix the gold luster dust in a paint palette with the alcohol or clear extract (see page 29). Carefully paint the cake stand, ensuring it does not get on the cookie base.

9. Pipe some royal icing onto the back of a mini rosette and adhere it to the top left corner of the cake.

10. Fit a piping bag with the leaf tip and fill with piping-consistency pale green icing. Pipe leaves on either side of the flower. Allow the details to completely dry for at least 6 hours prior to packaging.

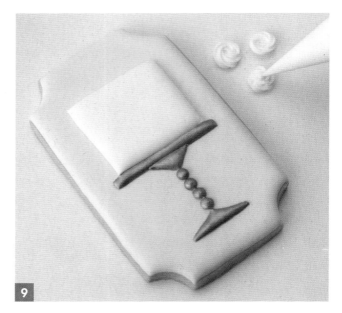

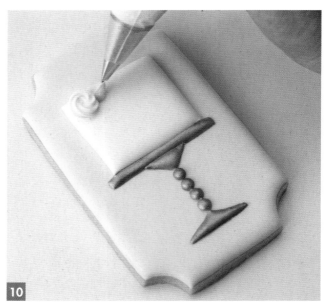

# BONUS PROJECTS: REPURPOSING COOKIE CUTTERS

Just because a season has come and gone doesn't mean you have to put away those specialty cookie cutters. Repurpose them to create something fresh and innovative for other occasions. Simply rotating a cutter sideways or upside down allows you to see it in a new way and create a totally different design. To discover the potential in a cutter, sketch or print a design you want to create and place it under a similarly shaped cutter to see if you can make it work. You may have to modify the design to fit the cutter, but that's part of the creative process. In these bonus projects, you'll use a pumpkin cookie cutter to create an elephant and Santa Claus.

## ELEPHANT

Simply turn the pumpkin-shaped cookies upside down and you have an elephant with a trunk!

**Note:** Very little black and white icings are needed for this design, so make a small amount.

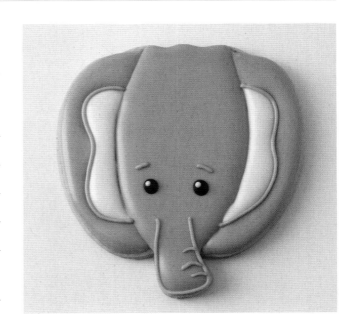

### MATERIALS

Baked and cooled pumpkin-shaped cookies

Edible food pen, light brown

Tipless piping bags

Flood-consistency royal icing, gray (see page 47)

Medium-consistency royal icing, light pink gray, black, and white (see page 47)

Scribe tool

*(continued)*

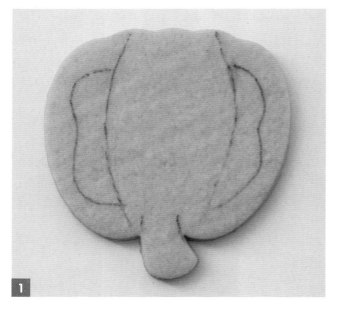

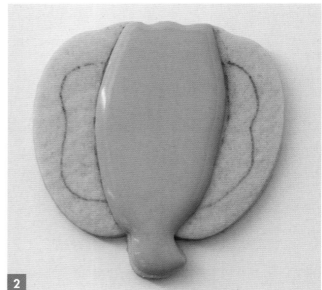

1. Flip the cookies upside down. Use an edible food pen to create an outline of the face and ears. I prefer to use a light brown pen as there is less risk of the ink seeping into the light-colored icing.

2. Fill tipless piping bags with all the icings (see page 50). Use the medium-consistency gray icing to outline and flood-consistency to fill the face. Allow the icing to crust over for at least 30 minutes before moving on to the next step. Be careful while handling the cookie, as it is still wet.

3. Outline and flood the inner ear with medium-consistency light pink icing. Let the cookie crust over for at least 30 minutes before moving on to step 4.

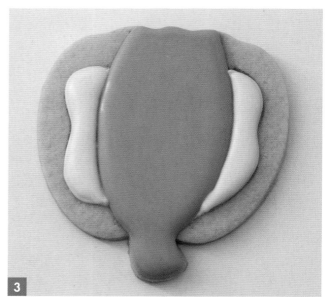

4. Outline and flood the outer ear with medium-consistency gray icing. Allow the fully iced cookie base dry for at least 6 hours before piping on facial details. Note that the base is not completely dry at this point, so be mindful while handling the cookie.

5. After the base has dried for at least 6 hours, use medium-consistency gray icing to pipe an outline around the ear, trunk, and brows. Lastly, pipe on two small black dots for the eyes, then immediately pipe smaller white reflections into the eyes using the medium-consistency icing and the wet-on-wet technique (see page 58). (You can use a scribe tool to mark the placement of the eyes first, if desired.) See finished cookie, page 151.

# SANTA CLAUS

Turn the pumpkin-shaped cookies on their side and you have Santa Claus with a pom-pom on his hat!

**Note:** Very little black icing is needed for this design, so make a small amount.

### MATERIALS

Baked and cooled
pumpkin-shaped cookies

Edible food pen, light brown

Tipless piping bags

Flood-consistency royal icing,
flesh color, red, and white
(see page 47)

Medium-consistency royal
icing, flesh color, red, white,
and black (see page 47)

Scribe tool

1. Rotate the pumpkin cutter to the left. Using an edible food pen, draw an outline of the hat and face.

*(continued)*

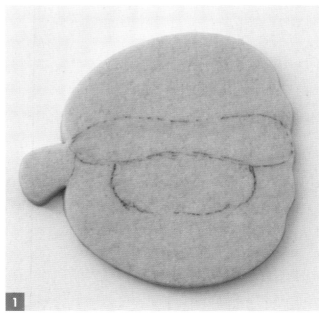

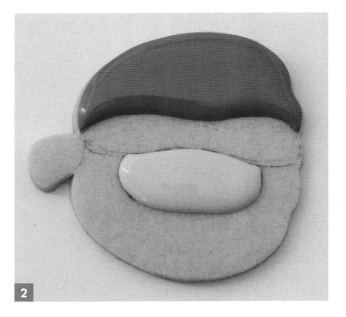

**2.** Fill tipless piping bags with all of the icings
(see page 50). Use the medium-consistency flesh
color to outline and flood the facial area. Then
use medium-consistency red icing to outline and
flood-consistency to fill the top of the hat. If the
cookie is smaller, use a medium-consistency for the
hat. Let these areas crust over for at least 30 minutes
before moving on to the next sections.

**3.** Use medium-consistency white icing to outline
and flood-consistency white icing to fill the beard.
If the cookie is on the smaller side, use a medium-
consistency for both outline and flood. Allow to crust
over for at least 30 minutes. Be careful while handling
the cookie as the other sections are not fully dry.

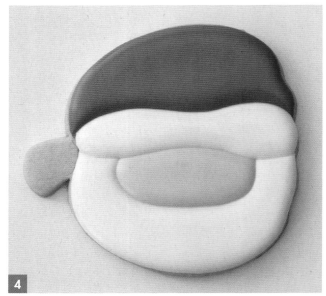

**4.** Use the medium-consistency white icing to outline
and flood the brim of the hat. Allow the cookie to
completely dry for at least 8 to 12 hours prior
to moving on to the next step.

**5.** Use medium-consistency flesh color icing for the nose. Use the medium-consistency white icing for the brows. Pipe on two small black dots for the eyes with medium-consistency black icing, then immediately pipe smaller white reflections into the eyes using the medium-consistency white icing and the wet-on-wet technique (see page 58). (You can use a scribe tool to mark the placement of the eyes first, if desired.) Ice the pom-pom with medium-consistency white icing. Let the nose dry for 1 hour prior to piping on the moustache.

**6.** Using medium-consistency white icing, pipe one side of the moustache and allow to completely crust over for at least 30 minutes.

**7.** Pipe the opposite side of the moustache. The cookie is now complete and should fully dry for at least 6 hours prior to packaging (see finished cookie, page 153).

# RESOURCES

For all the supplies, tools, and products featured in this book, visit: emmassweets.ca

# ACKNOWLEDGMENTS

To my husband, Rudy, my biggest supporter through my entire cookie journey. I would not be where I am today without the love and support you give me. I would never have participated in Food Network's Christmas Cookie Challenge because I was so terrified. I would never have taught classes because I thought I wasn't good enough. I would never have started an online shop because I was worried about how people would respond. And writing this book may not have come to fruition either, but it was you who encouraged me to go for it. You are more confident in my abilities than I am most days, and I thank you for that. I love you and appreciate you being by my side as I continue to move forward, wherever this journey leads.

To my daughter, Emma. You are bold, strong-willed, and confident. From the moment you were born, right up until today, you have a spark of tenacity that motivates me! Just like your brother and father, you are always encouraging me and supporting me to keep doing what I love. Whether you are taste-testing my cookies or telling me I am doing amazing, you are always by my side. I love you so much, Bella; don't ever change.

To my son, Aidan. You are wise beyond your years and have the most brilliant mind. You are always encouraging me and telling me how much you love what I do. You enjoy when I bake you fresh gingerbread cookies, even in the middle of the summer! And you know I will always do that for you because "I'll never say no to my baby." You have watched my videos and tell me I am the best cookie maker. Just the fact that you take an interest in what I do means so much to me. I love you more than you will ever know.

To my mother, Frances. I can clearly remember you making us Smarties cakes for our birthdays as children. They were bright, colorful, and cheerful and were my favorite back then. I would take the red Smarties off the cake and apply them to my lips to make red lipstick! Although you don't bake cakes anymore, I know you enjoy baking Italian cookies and fresh breads. What I have learned over the last few years from you is to never give up and to keep trying until I get it right. I know you are proud of me and everything I have accomplished.

To my sister, Nancy. You are always cheering me on from the sidelines. When I first started decorating cookies, you took all of my photos, edited them, and watermarked them for me. I didn't know how to use a camera back then, let alone create a watermark for my photos! You have been by my side throughout this entire journey, encouraging me and talking me through some bumps in the road. When I wanted to call it quits and give up, you helped me work out those emotions. Thanks for being there for me, Nance.

To my nephews, Maxim and Sebastian. You are both my little taste testers and cookie monsters! Every time I see you, the first thing you say is, "Zia, do you have any cookies for me?" When you saw me on TV, the excitement you both showed was heartwarming and so sweet. I know you will forever be my biggest fans and I love you both for your enthusiasm for my cookies!

To my father, Orlando. When I mentioned to you that I was going to write this book, the first thing you said was "do you know how to do that?" I said no at that time, but I did it! I know you are very proud of my accomplishments, even though you show it in your own way. Thank you for building me my workspace. There aren't many around with the talents and skills you possess.

To my brother, John (Gio). When I was making custom cookies, you would always refer me to your friends. In your own way, I know you support me and I appreciate that.

To my grandmother (*Nonina*) Maria. Although you are no longer with us, I know you are looking down on me and so proud of what I am doing today. As a little girl, I would sit in your small kitchen just watching you work your magic in front of your stove. You made amazing meals to feed your large family and always put so much love into it. You made the best sponge cakes! I don't recall ever seeing you use a recipe; rather, you just tossed everything together and produced consistent results every single time! I still cannot do that and

don't know if I ever could, but that's okay. You are missed and will forever be in my heart. I love you.

To my friend, Rose C. I have known you for many years, ever since I was a teenager. You have always been a positive and uplifting soul. You have a calming presence that is always reassuring. After making you a cake and cookies for your first pregnancy, you inspired me to start a social media page and suggested I start up a business selling my sweets. Despite my self-doubt, I went for it! You played a huge role in this more than you may even know. Had you not encouraged me to put myself out there at that exact moment, I don't know how things would have turned out. Thank you for your kind words and for just being you. The world is a better place because of you.

# ABOUT THE AUTHOR

**Mary Valentino** founded Emma's Sweets in 2013. She named the business after her daughter, Emma, who has a love for anything sweet! Prior to starting her part-time custom cookie business, Mary learned everything there was to know about royal icing and sugar cookies. Spending countless hours researching, taking courses, reading blogs, and purchasing recipes and tutorials online, she was determined to perfect the craft. But it didn't come easy at first, and there were a lot of failures and low points along the way. It was with the encouragement of family and friends that she pushed through and came out stronger every single time.

Mary currently resides in Ontario, Canada, along with her husband Rudy and her children, Emma and Aidan. She operates a successful online shop that has everything you need to get started on your cookie-decorating journey, including top-of-the-line baking supplies from around the globe, unique cookie cutters, and so much more. Not only does Mary provide amazing products and superior customer service, but she also produces content on how to decorate cookies on her social media platforms. During the past eight years, Mary has gained over 350K followers on all of her platforms combined. She continues to remain humble and grateful to each and every person who supports her but doesn't dismiss that all has come with hard work and determination.

At this time, Mary doesn't know what is next in her journey, but she is excited to see where it all leads!

# INDEX

Brimming with creative inspiration, how-to projects, and useful information to enrich your everyday life, Quarto.com is a favorite destination for those pursuing their interests and passions.

© 2022 Quarto Publishing Group USA Inc.
Text and images © 2022 Mary Valentino
Photography © 2022 Quarto Publishing Group USA Inc.

First Published in 2022 by Quarry Books, an imprint of The Quarto Group,
100 Cummings Center, Suite 265-D, Beverly, MA 01915, USA.
T (978) 282-9590 F (978) 283-2742 Quarto.com

Quarry Books titles are also available at discount for retail, wholesale, promotional, and bulk purchase. For details, contact the Special Sales Manager by email at specialsales@quarto.com or by mail at The Quarto Group, Attn: Special Sales Manager, 100 Cummings Center, Suite 265-D, Beverly, MA 01915, USA.

10 9 8 7 6 5 4 3 2 1

ISBN: 978-0-7603-7443-6

Digital edition published in 2022
eISBN: 978-0-7603-7444-3

Library of Congress Cataloging-in-Publication Data

Names: Valentino, Mary, author.
Title: The beginner's guide to cookie decorating : easy techniques and
   expert tips for designing and icing colorful treats / Mary Valentino.
Description: Beverly, MA : Quarry Books, 2022. | Includes index. | Summary:
   "The Beginner's Guide to Cookie Decorating shows how easy it is to make
   beginner-friendly, beautifully decorated cookies like the pros using
   easy techniques for icing, coloring, and designing. Discover the latest
   tips, tricks, and recipes from top cookie decorator Mary Valentino of
   Emma's Sweets"-- Provided by publisher.
Identifiers: LCCN 2021059902 | ISBN 9780760374436 (trade paperback) | ISBN
   9780760374443 (ebook)
Subjects: LCSH: Cookies. | Icings (Confectionery) | Baking. | Seasonal
   cooking. | LCGFT: Cookbooks.
Classification: LCC TX772 .V25 2022 | DDC 641.86/54--dc23/eng/20211216
LC record available at https://lccn.loc.gov/2021059902

Design: Kate Frances Design
Cover Images: Mary Valentino
Page Layout and Design: Megan Jones Design
Photography: Mary Valentino except by Amy Vee Photography on pages 2, 6, 7, and 157

Printed in China